Game Design Deep Dive

Game Design Critic Joshua Bycer is back with another entry in the Game Design Deep Series to focus on the youngest genre yet: soulslikes. Over a decade, From Software defined a new genre that has led to studios chasing after them hit after hit. In this book, Josh will cover the history of the genre and popular soulslike games of the 2010s and discuss what aspects of design make a game a soulslike.

- The first book looking at the history of the genre
- A breakdown of both action and RPG design for fans and designers of both
- A lesson on difficulty in games and why harder doesn't mean better

Joshua Bycer is a Game Design Critic with more than 7 years of experience critically analyzing game design and the industry itself. In that time through Game-Wisdom.com, he has interviewed hundreds of game developers and members of the industry about what it means to design video games.

Game Design Deep Dive
Soulslike

Joshua Bycer

CRC Press
Taylor & Francis Group
Boca Raton London New York

CRC Press is an imprint of the
Taylor & Francis Group, an **informa** business

First edition published 2024
by CRC Press
2385 NW Executive Center Drive, Suite 320, Boca Raton FL 33431

and by CRC Press
4 Park Square, Milton Park, Abingdon, Oxon, OX14 4RN

CRC Press is an imprint of Taylor & Francis Group, LLC

ISBN: 978-1-032-58439-3 (hbk)
ISBN: 978-1-032-58115-6 (pbk)
ISBN: 978-1-003-45007-8 (ebk)

DOI: 10.1201/9781003450078

Typeset in Minion
by codeMantra

Contents

Acknowledgments

For each *Game Design Deep Dive*, I run a donation incentive for people to donate to earn an acknowledgment in each one of my upcoming books. I would like to thank the following people for supporting my work while I was writing this book.

- Michael Berthaud
- Ben Bishop
- DS
- Jason Ellis
- Jake Everitt
- Thorn Falconeye
- Puppy Games
- Luke Hughes
- Adriaan Jansen
- Jonathan Ku
- Aron Linde
- Josh Mull
- NWDD
- Rey Obomsawin
- Janet Oblinger
- Onslaught
- David Pittman

Social Media

Social Media Contacts

- Email: gamewisdombusiness@gmail.com
- My YouTube channel where I post daily design videos and developer interview: youtube.com/c/game-wisdom
- Main site: Game-Wisdom.com
- Twitter: Twitter.com/GWBycer

Additional Books

If you enjoyed this entry and want to learn more about design, you can read my other works:

20 Essential Games to Study – A high-level look at 20 unique games that are worth studying their design to be inspired by or for a historical look at the game industry.

Game Design Deep Dive: Platformers – The first entry in the *Game Design Deep Dive* series focusing on 2D and 3D platformer designs. A top-to-bottom discussion of the history, mechanics, and design of the game industry's most recognizable and long-lasting genre.

Game Design Deep Dive: Roguelikes – The second entry in the *Game Design Deep Dive* series focusing on the rise and design of roguelike games. A look back at how the genre started, what makes the design unique, and an across-the-board discussion on how it has become the basis for new designs by modern developers.

Game Design Deep Dive: Horror – The third entry in the *Game Design Deep Dive* series examining the philosophy and psychology behind horror. Looking at the history of the genre, I explored what it means to create a scary game or use horror elements in any genre.

Game Design Deep Dive: F2P – The fourth entry in the *Game Design Deep Dive* series, focusing on the mobile and live service genre. Besides looking at the history and design of these games, I also talked about the ethical ramifications of their monetization systems.

Game Design Deep Dive: Trading and Collectible Card Games – The fifth entry in the *Game Design Deep Dive* series, which looks at the deck building genre along with CCGs and TCG design, as well as covering the balancing that goes into designing cards and sets.

All my books are available from major retailers and from Taylor & Francis directly.

Preface

I've been wanting to write an entry in this series that focused on reflex-driven design and to discuss the nature of difficulty in games, and soulslikes provided me the opportunity to do both. Breaking down difficulty in games is one of the harder aspects of game analysis and is exceptionally important when we're talking about any kind of game. When it comes to reflex-driven design, this book is going to act as the precursor to discussing it in length with shooters and action games later, but it was great for me to start putting to words about how important responsiveness and feedback are to these games.

I hope everyone will get something out of this, and to hopefully move the conversation forward when it comes to difficulty and challenge in games.

1 Introduction

1.1 The Goal of This Book

For this series, it's time to turn to a genre that in one decade became popular, started a new game design trend, and the top of the genre still resides with the company that popularized it (Figure 1.1). The **soulslike** genre is a name that doesn't quite describe what it is, and yet unlike the term **Metroidvania**, no one has to question it.

In this book, we're going to discuss the specific details that make a game a soulslike thanks to the games that popularized it and the ones that have been chasing those successes. As I'll talk about in the next section, soulslikes represent a subgenre that exists between action and **RPG**, and I will be covering the relevant details.

By the time this book is published, my entry focusing on RPG design will have been published, which will cover a lot of the basics and foundational elements of the gameplay. However, there hasn't been an entry yet that has gone into detail about action design, and this book will begin exploring the concepts of creating action gameplay, along with a study on environmental and level design.

DOI: 10.1201/9781003450078-1

Figure 1.1

Welcome to a book all about playing challenging video games, and I couldn't think of anything more perfect to start with than the image that every person who has played these games has seen before.

Each book tends to have one subject that stands out in terms of what I'm going to cover, and for this one, that's going to be about difficulty design. The souls-like genre succeeded thanks to a very specific approach to difficulty, and it's one aspect that developers trying to make their own, and consumers who defend these games tend to not understand said approach.

Finally, I'll break down the major aspects of From Software's latest hit at the time of drafting this book: *Elden Ring*, to talk about what it could mean for the genre going forward.

1.2 The Subgenre Situation

If you're reading the "Game Design Deep Dive" series in order, this is the first time that I'm covering a subgenre in the game industry, and that means that the structure of this book is going to be different compared to the genre-focused ones. Soulslikes by their design are a mix of action and RPG gameplay, or reflex-driven and abstracted design, respectively. Both individual genres are very dense in terms of what goes into them (Figure 1.2). The entry on general RPG design has been the longest book I've written currently. By contrast, this may be one of the shorter entries, as the genre itself is the "youngest" out of all the ones I've covered so far.

What this means for you reading this is that there will be overlapping discussions about action and RPG design in this book where it pertains to soulslikes, just as there will be aspects of both designs that will not be discussed in full.

Figure 1.2

Soulslikes could not exist without the evolution of action and RPG design over the 2000s and how both genres began taking elements from one another.

Depending on how many subgenres I tackle in the future, especially of the different kinds of RPGs, this situation will pop up again.

For a more comprehensive look at RPG design, please read *Game Design Deep Dive: Roleplaying Games*, and hopefully in the future, a later Deep Dive focusing on the action genre.

2

The Proto Soulslike Era

2.1 The *King's Field* Series

Fans of the soulslike genre obviously know developer From Software from one of the many hits they released in the 2010s (and what I'll be going over later in this book). Older fans may know them for the cult classic *Armored Core* series (first released in 1997), and it has a new entry from the studio in 2023. But From Software's debut game was only released in Japan in 1994: *King's Field* (Figure 2.1).

The *King's Field* series is not what we would consider a soulslike, and therefore will not be covered at length here. Each entry is a first-person action RPG taking place in a different fantasy land. The very first entry was never ported outside of Japan, and US audiences' first experience would be *King's Field 2* released in 1995. All four entries (#3 released in 1996 and #4 released in 2001) would embody the same design and mechanics. The player explored and fought entirely in first person looking for clues, equipment, and the items needed to make progress.

One aspect that we can draw parallels from *King's Field* to the soulslike was a focus on a specific form of real-time combat. Every weapon in the game had different stats related to damage, but also a different way of being swung by the player's character. If the weapon does not connect with the enemy's body or **hitbox,**

DOI: 10.1201/9781003450078-2

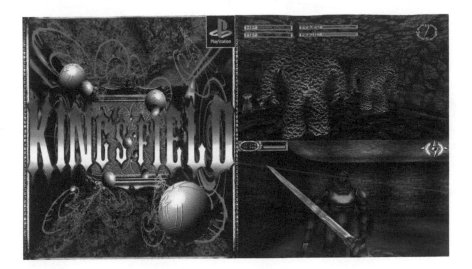

Figure 2.1

King's Field was From Software's first franchise that hasn't been seen in a long time, but it's anyone's guess what their next project will be.

then the attack doesn't count as a hit. The player can only do maximum damage with their weapon when their stamina bar is refilled after each swing. This had the impact of slowing down combat and requiring the player to properly time the swings of their attacks; an aspect that would be refined when I discuss later soulslikes.

The reason why many people like to compare *King's Field* as the start of the soulslike trend is thanks to its difficulty and focus on exploration. Each game leaves it up to the player to explore and try to figure things out on their own (Figure 2.2). It is quite possible to die within the first minute of starting a game due to environmental hazards or wandering into an enemy that the player cannot fight yet. The high difficulty and huge game spaces earned the series a following, and From Software would continue with another series with a similar design: *Shadow Tower* and *Shadow Tower: Abyss* released in 1998 and 2003, respectively.

2.2 The Limitations of Early 3D

The 90s, specifically, the mid-90s, was not a favorable time for early consoles and the action genre when technology allowed for 3D and first-person designs. With the PlayStation released in 1994, the launch did not have a controller that allowed for easy 3D controls. The use of analog sticks would become popularized thanks to Nintendo with the Nintendo 64 released in 1996. Before that, consoles that tried to use three-dimensional movement would only have the directional pad, or D-pad, for movement (Figure 2.3). To control the camera, developers had to figure out workarounds like having a button press that holding it would allow

Figure 2.2

The feeling of being a stranger in a strange land and having to explore and find your bearings has been the start of many of From Software's games and where *Dark Souls* began.

Figure 2.3

The evolution of controller design is a fascinating one for how it impacted game design. The original PlayStation 1 controller has similarities to the Super Nintendo gamepad, but as the demand for 3D increased, controllers needed to change, and the DualShock is now considered the standard layout in terms of buttons and gamepad functionality to this day.

for "turning", while normal movement would make the character strafe around. For many first-person perspective games released on consoles at this time, the act of controlling them was a nightmare compared to the ease of using a keyboard and mouse for PC games.

Early games released on the PlayStation, and failed consoles like the 3DO and Jaguar (both released in 1993) had to make use of the limited console technology. It wouldn't be until the Sega Dreamcast released in 1999 that a console would be on par with arcade hardware, and later platforms would overtake the arcade. For the mid-90s, early 3D games had poor frames per second, or FPS, which limited how much action could be performed at one time. Due to how hardware-intensive these games were, many of them would feature plain or nonexistent backgrounds to cut down on the number of elements that needed to be rendered on screen. For the games that didn't do that, they often had very low framerates. While gamers today complain if a game is only at 30 FPS, many early 3D games ran at 15 or less FPS. As developers became more familiar with the hardware, later PS1 games would run better and be able to show more things on screen, and then the jump in quality in the 2000s saw far more impressive 3D technology.

Returning to the gamepad itself, while Nintendo did popularize the use of an analog stick for 3D movement, the practice would not become fully adopted among other console releases until the Sega Dreamcast. Sony did release an updated controller for the PlayStation 1, dubbed the DualShock in 1997. This design would become the basis for all future Sony controllers as the DualShock was iterated on with each new PlayStation. Nintendo's solution was to use four buttons: the C Buttons, on the Nintendo 64 for camera manipulation, which worked but did not provide the same fidelity as a second analog stick. The DualShock presented what has since been adopted as the standard for gamepad design – featuring two analog sticks that are meant to be controlled by both thumbs. The left analog stick specifically controls movement; the right analog stick manipulates the camera (Figure 2.4).

This setup allowed someone to move the character and camera independently from one another and would lead to Bungie releasing one of the most popular first-person shooters with *Halo* released in 2001 and the banner game for Microsoft's Xbox system released at the same time. Because the gamepad directly impacts what buttons and layouts are available for that platform, no company is in any rush to try and create a competing one. Nintendo ran into this issue when it came to having ports of series released on their different platforms in the past, as the different layouts would interfere with being able to control these games as easily as being on a Sony or Microsoft platform.

There is a lot more to discuss with regard to the evolution of action design that I will save for the Deep Dive which focuses on the genre. To relate this to the soulslike genre, besides the changes to game design philosophy in the 2000s, there was no way that the consoles in the 90s could have anything near the same level of depth as *Demon's Souls*, or any soulslike for that matter.

Figure 2.4

After the move to 3D, gamepad design has become fully standardized among the PlayStation and Xbox layouts, and we will not see any new designs from either company, as that would impact all games being developed for their platforms.

3

The Basics of
Action Design

3.1 Defining Reflex-Driven Design

This is the first time in the Deep Dive series that I'm able to focus on action, or reflex-driven, gameplay (Figure 3.1). As I said at the start, with soulslikes being a combination of both action and RPG design, it is important to understand the basics of both genres if you want to have any attempt at being able to make one. These next two chapters are going to be primers for both genres, but I do want to emphasize that there is far more to the design and balancing of both that are separate from making a soulslike that are in their respective genre books.

Reflex-driven games represent all titles that focus on the player's reaction time and control to dictate success or failure. Even with games that added in RPG progression **systems** which will be discussed in the next chapter, if the player is not good enough at the game, no amount of abstracted progression will save them in reflex-driven games. Easy examples would be the platformer, shooter, and fighting game genres.

During the 2000s, reflex-driven design reached its peak among the mainstream consoles and platforms with the likes of *Devil May Cry* (released in 2001 by Capcom), competitive shooters like *Unreal Tournament* (released in 1999 by

DOI: 10.1201/9781003450078-3

9

Figure 3.1

Reflex-driven design is all about the player's ability to control and react determining whether they will win. Even if there are some RPG elements to it, the focus is always on the player to dictate the outcome.

Epic Games and Digital Extremes), and many others. With the problems of early 3D solved that I mentioned in Section 2.2, designers were free to design ever increasingly difficult action games. The genre has always had a dedicated fanbase, but it also showed the limitations of the design.

Reflex-driven gameplay is entirely focused on the player's own skill level. It wouldn't be until the mid-2010s that more designers looked at approachability options (a topic I'll return to in Section 7.3) to lessen the demand on the player. Many action titles are known for having extremely high **skill floors** that would quickly thin out the consumer base from the ones who could rise to the challenge, and the ones who couldn't (Figure 3.2). People who play challenging action games will often do what they can to master them, with designers regularly having an optional harder mode for people who want to test their skills. The act of designing around mastery is something exclusive to action design that I want to point out here, but it is not related directly to soulslike, and why I won't be talking about it in this book.

When approaching an action-focused game, it requires a different knowledge base compared to an RPG or abstracted design. One of the most important aspects is getting "the feel" of the gameplay right in the player's hands. This is a combination of the **UI** or "user interface," the responsiveness of the character, and how both are balanced with the enemies and obstacles in your game. People who play action games at a high level can quickly figure out if the game's feel is working or not, and having a reflex-driven game with a poor feel will repel

Figure 3.2

The 2000s gave us a decade of some of the most well-received action games and franchises that are still around to this day.

consumers. The other sections in this chapter will talk about some of the common aspects of action games and how they relate to feel.

One of the differences between purely reflex-driven design and soulslikes is trying to create a fixed character control. In an action game, characters will often attack as fast as the player can input buttons, with advanced games having commands that can be triggered in the span of milliseconds. Section 3.3 will cover the use of input buffering and how it has been used to slow down combat and put everyone on an equal footing.

3.2 UI Fundamentals

An essential aspect of making a proper action game is getting the UI right. More than anything else, if your game doesn't feel right in the player's hands, then all the story, all the development, and all the work you put into it will not matter. Understanding UI is a very important topic and one that differs from genre to genre.

Due to the reflex-driven nature of soulslikes and action design, figuring out the proper control scheme of your game is crucial (Figure 3.3). To start with, the first concept you need to grasp is the "standard" or "neutral" position that someone is holding a gamepad or sitting at a computer. Thanks to gamepads becoming standardized, you will not have to worry about different platforms having vastly different designs. With that said however, if you are building your game with accessibility in mind, there are controllers specifically designed for people who cannot use a normal controller, and there are resources out there to learn more about the

Figure 3.3

Part of what made soulslikes more appealing compared to traditional action games, was reducing the number of inputs and advanced commands needed to play them, and this will be discussed more in Chapter 8.

topic, such as the organization Ablegamers. For the general consumer, they are going to be holding a gamepad with their left thumb on the left analog stick, the right thumb on either the right analog stick or resting on one of the face buttons, and their index fingers on the left and right shoulder buttons respectively. For keyboards, the standard movement keys and neutral positions are often focused on the WSAD keys for a person's left hand, with the pinky finger on shift and the left thumb on the spacebar and holding the mouse with their right hand.

To build a good UI for an action game, you need to understand the differences between primary and secondary mechanics and how they relate to button placement. Primary mechanics are the commands that a player is going to be performing constantly every second of playing the game. If we were talking about a platformer, "jumping" would be a primary mechanic. Secondary mechanics are those that occur less frequently and/or situational actions. A few examples would be opening a door, drinking a health potion, or sitting down on a bench.

Primary mechanics in your game should always be given one of the buttons that the consumer can reach from the neutral position. Every primary mechanic should not share its button with another primary or secondary mechanic. The reason is that the more commands tied to a single button, the harder it becomes to tell the game to perform the correct action at the right time. Famous examples of this came from the open world genre where designers would put the "climb down carefully" command on the same button as "dive forward," and if the character was not precisely in the right spot, they would tumble over an edge instead of a climb down.

Figure 3.4

For the longest time, the adventure genre would use multiple commands to represent all the verbs that someone could do in the game, but this was often just complexity for complexity's sake. Adventure games designed today use fewer verbs or just a context sensitive command.

Secondary mechanics can share button assignments and are often tied to what is known as a "context sensitive command." What this simply means is that a command can only be activated in a specific context, and there is no possibility that the player will want to do something else at this exact moment. A simple example is the ubiquitous "use" command. Use, in this context, can mean anything – pull a lever, open a jar, search a cabinet, and so on. As a designer, you do not need to set up multiple buttons to specifically open a door, close a door, open a cabinet, or search a cabinet, when all that could be tied to just one input and one universal command (Figure 3.4).

What commands you place next to each other on either your keyboard or your gamepad is also a factor in your UI. Mis pressing a button can happen very regularly, and you don't want to put very situational options next to each other like the "sneak very carefully" command next to the "throw a very loud grenade" command.

Another important concept to understand when building a UI is the use of affordances. An affordance in this respect is using something natural to help add a secondary association when remembering what a button does. A simple, and yet pivotal, example of this is tying "driving" or "shooting" to the trigger buttons on a gamepad. The act of pushing in the trigger is of course related to the act of pushing down on a pedal or pulling a trigger. Another example that was used was the "paper doll UI" that was popularized by the *Assassin's Creed* series (first released in 2007 by Ubisoft Montreal). With it, the character's leg commands

Figure 3.5

The hook of the *Grand Theft Auto* series is being able to do vastly different activities all in a single game. For each gameplay system, it required the designers to make their own UI and control scheme.

were tied to the bottom face button, arms to the middle two, and looking (or the head) commands to the top face button. One affordance that I personally like to use is to make sure that similar primary commands are set up to be used by the same hand. For instance, if I'm moving a character with my left hand, I like to map any kind of movement or dodging abilities to the left trigger or left button, so I know that left=movement. Again, this is going to be highly dependent on what primary and secondary mechanics are in your title.

The more commands you need to tie to buttons, the harder it is going to be to hit everything from the neutral position. One key component of good UI design is to keep the player from having to constantly shift their hands around or put their fingers in awkward positions. As an example, if the player needs to hold down the right or top face button to run, but they also need to be controlling the camera with the right analog stick, the only way to do both is to shift their right hand so that their index finger is hitting the face buttons at the same time they are moving the stick with their right thumb. If you're not used to this, try it out yourself and see how long you can keep your hand in this position before it starts to cramp and hurt.

There are some ways to get around having more commands than easy-to-reach keys. One is to require the player to shift their hands and use this for specific situations or when the game changes. For a series like *Grand Theft Auto* by Rockstar North (first released in 1997) when the player is running around on foot and driving different vehicles, how they control the on-foot sections is different from when they are driving, so the UI for both modes is different (Figure 3.5).

3. The Basics of Action Design

Another option is to build your UI around having a "modifier" button. When the player is holding the modifier down, all the buttons have different commands associated with them, such as having a modifier to start sneaking around or activating a different form of move set.

3.3 The Importance of Input Buffering

An area where soulslikes differentiate from pure action games is by forcing the player to conform to the pacing and speed of the combat system. When compared to other action games, every soulslike is noticeably slower in terms of character animations. Instead of this being viewed as "clunky" or "slow," fans have come to enjoy the more grounded pacing of these games, and that is facilitated by using input buffering.

When someone plays a videogame, the game is constantly checking for inputs from the player – if the player hits the jump button, then the character should jump. In games where there is no input buffering, the game will only read inputs when the character is able to accept them. If the player hits the attack button three times in a row, but the other two pushes occur while the attack animation is being played out, the game will not perform the other two attacks. This is where a lot of action games tend to favor button mashing so that the player's commands are done immediately when the game starts reading inputs again.

What input buffering does is that while a character is performing an action and the animation is playing, the game is still checking for inputs. In this example, if the player hits the attack button during an animation, the game will queue, or "buffer" the input so that when the character is responsive again, they will automatically perform whatever action that was queued (Figure 3.6).

Input buffering is often used in fighting games to queue up combo attacks that would otherwise be too fast to input on reaction. For soulslikes, this serves an important purpose in restricting the combat pacing and flow to exactly what the designers intend. In these games, just being faster with your hands would not give you an advantage during combat, as every single character must abide by the animations for every move. By using input buffering, the character will respond with the next command the absolute moment that they are finished with the previous one.

This also makes combat smooth to experience, as the player can get a handle on the speed of how enemies and other characters behave – a heavy enemy will naturally swing their weapons slower than someone using lighter weapons. In a way, input buffering acts as a method to reduce the reflex-driven skills needed to play a soulslike and has since been adopted by every designer making one.

From a design standpoint, there isn't much more to discuss, as the implementation of input buffering is going to fall on the programming side. The one detail you do need to keep in mind if you want to add input buffering to your game is the window in which the game will be checking for inputs. If the timing window is too small, the game may not pick up on a player's input if they did it immediately after the initial animation has begun. If it's too long, then it may pick up an

Figure 3.6

Input buffering is essential in soulslikes to keep the pacing and flow at a specific rate. For fighting games, this is integral to their entire system of combos and chaining attacks together. Instead of the player having to time attacks directly to the animation, it's more about inputting the commands in the correct sequence, and the animation is not factored into the timing (with exception of juggling the opponent).

accidental button press. A good period to check for inputs is during the actual animation – swinging the sword, dodging the attack, etc. Due to the nature of these games, the actual animations you will create for them will have an impact on the design, balancing, and pacing of the game, and I will discuss this more in Section 8.3.

3.4 Common Combat Mechanics and Terminology

Action game design has a variety of unique mechanics and terms associated with it that are important to understand if you want to build any reflex-driven game. I'm only covering the relevant elements that are also related to soulslike design and save the rest for a future Deep Dive.

Action games are about a combination of offense and defensive moves, with parallels to the fighting game genre. One aspect that soulslikes have popularized that was not featured in action design previously was the use of an "action limiter." In action games prior to soulslikes, characters could dodge as much as they wanted, attack as much as they wanted, and just be as reactive as the player wanted (Figure 3.7). As part of the design of creating a slower pace combat, soulslikes adopted the use of stamina as a limitation that was in a lot of real-time dungeon crawlers. Every command the player can do has a stamina cost; if the

3. The Basics of Action Design

Figure 3.7

The 2000s action game market was all about high-speed play with a focus on mastering the many different combos and means of attacking, such as in *Bayonetta* (released in 2009 by Platinum Games).

character is out of stamina, they are unable to perform commands until the bar recharges enough to start doing things again. As a form of balancing in souls-likes, lighter and faster weapons use less stamina, while heavier weapons meant to do far more damage come with a larger stamina drain. A character without stamina is a sitting duck, and this is why upgrading the amount of stamina for a character is one of the first upgrades players will invest in.

The next concept to discuss is the use of Invincibility Frames more commonly referred to as **I-Frames**. In games where the player is required to dodge a variety of attacks coming from all sides, designers will provide them with a universal defensive move that is designed to ignore damage. The I-Frame itself is a period during an animation where the player's hitbox does not recognize any incoming damage that hits it, hence becoming invincible. With that said, in most action games, this period is maybe a tenth of a second.

Here is an example of how this happens in one of the *Dark Souls* games by From Software. When the player hits the dodge command the character will perform the following animations:

1. The character begins to tuck into a rolling position.
2. The character's model starts rolling and their body is off the ground.
3. The character's model is rolling on the ground.
4. The character starts to stand up.
5. The character enters the neutral position or starts the next queued command.

Figure 3.8

It's impossible to show dodge timings in still pictures, but here are some different armor types in soulslikes. The image on the left is from *Dark Souls 3* with lighter armor, the middle is the famous "Havel" set from *Dark Souls 1*, which was the strongest and heaviest armor in the game. The image on the right is one of the heavy armor sets from *Nioh*. While *Nioh* does have a heavy-weight condition, you are still noticeably faster dodging in it compared to *Dark Souls*, but the enemies are far more active and dangerous.

During the second animation, the character is in an I-Frame position and cannot be hit by any incoming damage. Depending on the difficulty of the game and the duration of dodging, this maneuver could be reserved for advanced play, or just be required to have any chance at winning. While dodging does have its obvious advantages, due to the limited portion of the dodging animation where the character has I-Frames, it leaves them open to attack if they mistime the dodge, or if there are multiple attacks coming at different intervals.

In some games, the act of dodging will depend on the character's equipment weight – the heavier the armor they're wearing, the slower the roll is (Figure 3.8). How this works from an animation standpoint is that the character will take more time to get to the I-Frame portion of the animation and will have a slower recovery period; the actual I-Frames will be the same. In the *Dark Souls* games, the slowest roll is almost impossible to perfectly dodge some of the faster attacks in the game. In other soulslikes that I'll talk about later in this book, the distance the character can cover while dodging can be affected by their weight as well. This kind of balancing is used to differentiate combat styles between those who wear lighter armor and have less defense but can dodge easier, vs. those who are better at blocking and absorbing damage because their dodge is so slow.

3. The Basics of Action Design

Blocking is another form of defense featured in many action and fighting games. For the purpose here, blocking will require the player to equip their character with some kind of shield. Shields can have different resistances to different kinds of damage that impact how much an attack will affect their health. If the character is using a fire shield that resists 90% of incoming fire damage, and they block a 100-point fireball, then they will only take 10 points of damage. To provide a counter to blocking, whenever a character blocks an attack, it will drain a portion of their stamina in relation to the strength of the shield and the strength of the attack. This also provides a way of differentiating smaller shields from larger shields that block more but eat up more stamina with each one. If a character runs out of stamina while blocking, they may become stunned for a few seconds. Blocking is considered the safest defensive move the player has access to.

In contrast, the next example is the riskiest in the form of a parry or riposte action. Instead of blocking the attack, the character performs a parrying animation. If they catch the opponent's attack with their parry, the opposing attack is canceled, and the enemy becomes vulnerable to increased damage or a special counterattack. This maneuver is the riskiest defensive move to pull off as the punishment for failing means getting hit by the full force of the enemy's attack. The timing for the parry has a massive impact on the difficulty of the game and its practicality during combat. Some games have a very wide window: like half a second to a full second. Other games may use a small window, a tenth of a second or shorter, where the parry is active. The weapon or parrying equipment can also impact the length of time, with easier weapons having a longer parry window compared to harder ones. Another important consideration for parrying is whether or not the "parry" occurs the second the player hits the button or is there a slight animation delay. Having that delay greatly increases the difficulty of pulling it off, as the player must factor that in along with the timing of the enemy's attack.

Switching over to offensive moves, soulslikes typically feature fewer ways of attacking compared to full-action titles, in order to minimize the number of elements the player must keep in mind while playing. Many titles will have only a few attack commands – typically a normal and a heavy attack. Depending on the game, the player may be able to hold down one of the buttons to charge the attack to do more damage. One area where From Software's soulslikes have differed is with having one-handed vs. two-handed holds for weapons (Figure 3.9). Holding a weapon with one hand allows the player to use their shield while fighting. Holding the same weapon with two hands makes the weapon do more damage, could change the nature of the swings, but it also prevents them from easily blocking incoming attacks.

Part of the balance of using different weapons is providing a means to allow heavier weapons a chance of hitting. Typically, when a character is struck by an attack, it causes them to flinch and abruptly end whatever animation they're doing. In a lot of games, this can be done repeatedly and causes a "stun lock" – where the character can't do anything and is stuck in place while being attacked. To stop

Figure 3.9

From Software has done the best job in the soulslike market for providing multiple ways of building a character and fighting with them. Here, I'm using a one-handed flail with the two-handed hold to increase its damage and give me a better chance of staggering the boss.

enemies from being stun locked, they can be programmed to instantly recover after a specific number of attacks or make it so that incoming damage can't stop them from attacking. In the latter's case, it is important to provide the player with a way of being able to safely do damage to enemies like this, such as making their animations very slow and allowing a faster character to stick and move.

Against other players, being able to stun lock a player may be great for the one who is doing it but can be frustrating for someone who is unable to do anything and has led to the use of what is known as "super armor." For stronger attacks, the character doing it may get the property of super armor, which means that they will still take incoming damage, but it will not knock them out of the attack animation. If someone tries to run up and stop the attack, they'll find themselves still getting hit if they are in the way of the swing. Depending on the game, super armor may be countered if the attack is strong enough, but this is not set in stone.

A common element for both offensive and defensive moves is what is known as an animation cancel. In fighting games, this is used as a way for a player to chain attacks or actions that otherwise wouldn't be possible due to the length of each animation. Due to their importance and power, being able to cancel an animation is often tied to using up a character's special meter, or there may just be a limited number of times per round. For action games, their use is often tied to allowing the player to get out of an animation that they don't want to finish. Let's say an enemy starts performing an attack that can't be blocked while the player is already starting their attack animation. The standard form of canceling is a

3. The Basics of Action Design

Figure 3.10

Avoiding and mitigating damage is an instrumental part of any combat system and is needed if there are weapons of different attack speeds. In *Mortal Shell* on the left, the "harden" ability makes slow weapons viable by allowing you to block the hit and continue the attack, while *Elden Ring* allows canceling and balances the strength of the attack in relation to the weight of the weapon.

"dodge cancel" – by hitting the dodge button, the character will stop the animation they're in and immediately perform a dodge away. To balance this, the player cannot dodge cancel once the animation is committed: when the attack is connecting as an example. This is also important if the player is fighting fast enemies and/or those that cannot be interrupted while they are attacking (Figure 3.10). Without being able to cancel out of an animation, the player will not have any way to avoid damage from something faster or more reactive than their character. Advanced play in action games and shooters will often revolve around using animation cancel to cancel out the recovery or reloading animations – enabling the player to perform multiple attacks far quicker than normal. Like everything else when it comes to action design, the use and implementation of animation canceling will need to be balanced with the rest of your game.

An option that some designers like when they are trying to design a unique or noticeably harder encounter is to use what is known as "input reading." What happens is that the enemy AI is programmed to automatically perform certain actions if it detects a button press by the player. There are large and small examples of this, and they are all going to be dependent on the kind of game you are building. Some action games may punish the player for performing the same attacks in the same order by having the AI automatically block if it detects the same button presses. To counter grabs, the AI could be set up to use a grab cancel maneuver if it detects the grab button. Soulslikes may set up an enemy to be more aggressive if the player hits the button to heal as a way of punishing someone for trying to heal at the wrong time. The downside of input reading is that it can come across as an artificial way of making an enemy harder – that it's not about learning the enemy but about exploiting the fact that it will perform the same reaction every time.

There is far more to action game fundamentals and terminology, but these are the basics that soulslikes have used. When I talk about enemy design in Section 8.2, I'll discuss more about how these elements are filtered through the different kinds of enemies that can be in a game.

One final point before moving on, everything discussed in this chapter is not required to be in your game. Many different action and soulslike games have used some, all, or none of the elements featured here. Just like discussing the different systems and mechanics of RPG design in my Deep Dive on the genre, before you can start building your gameplay and systems out, you need to decide on what elements and mechanics you want to feature in your specific take on the genre. In Section 5.3 discussing the other soulslikes, you are going to see how vastly different each one is from one another and from the designs that From Software implemented.

3.5 An Intro to Action Balance

Balancing any reflex-driven game is very difficult to pull off if you are not familiar with the genre, and even then, it is going to be dependent on the skill level you are expecting out of your consumer base. The elements I mentioned in the last section all have different properties that impact how easy or hard they are to use. If you're building a very challenging action game, you may not implement any kind of blocking, or even dodging, and may rely solely on precise parrying. For someone making an easier game, they may only have blocking with very few restrictions on how much the player can use it. Some advanced examples may build their entire combat system around a singular form of defense.

A lot of the balancing that goes into reflex-driven games is going to be based on the enemies and obstacles that the player must get by. The more demanding they are on the player, the harder the game will become as a result. A common design trap for developers is either intentionally or unintentionally putting in a difficulty spike that catches players unaware, and a segment of the consumer base ends up quitting because of it (Figure 3.11).

What I'm going to be talking about in this section is just the absolute basics, and again, how they relate to the soulslike genre. A more in-depth discussion will be saved for when I talk about the action genre in full.

When you are looking at balancing an action game, the first areas you need to concern yourself with are how the character performs offensively and defensively. These are some of the questions you will need to answer:

Figure 3.11

From Software is infamous at this point for designing boss fights as skill checks in all their games. While writing this book, *Armored Core 6* was released and the game's Chapter 1 boss fight shown here, proved to be a massive wall for people to be forced to learn how to play the game.

- How well can the character fight?
- Are there enemies that the character cannot fight given their move set?
- Is the character too good at fighting?

When you are building your combat system, you need to figure out the extent of the character's move set – what actions can they perform during combat to fight? Different kinds of moves can be set up to handle different enemies. Having a heavy attack that specifically breaks an enemy's guard would be the perfect counter to enemies that are very defensive but wouldn't work on something that is constantly moving. For every enemy type in your game, including bosses, the character, and by extension the player, must have a suitable answer.

If the player can only rely on blocking as their form of defense, and you implement an enemy whose every attack is un-blockable, then the player can feel like the game is cheating if they have no means of fighting it. How you set up encounters with different enemy types also impacts the balance of your game. If your combat system is built entirely on close-ranged attacks, and a section is filled with nothing but long-range sniper-type enemies, that can be another pain point and difficulty spike. This is not the same as designing an enemy that specifically requires the player to use one part of their combat system over the other, such as an enemy that can't be hit with quick attacks but can be hit with heavy attacks or grabs.

Figure 3.12

One of the ways that action games differentiate themselves is by having different advanced ways of playing. In *Sifu* on the left, the game had an emphasis on different dodges that needed to be timed and aimed to avoid damage. *Furi* (released in 2016 by The Game Bakers) required mastering multiple offensive and defensive moves to have any chance of winning.

Just as you can make things too hard, you can also make things too easy for your intended audience. If the character can stun lock every enemy with no way for them to fight back or stop the player, then where is the challenge to keep someone playing? Again, this is going to be dependent on the skill level of the audience you are building your game around.

When you're building different attacks, weapons, skills, etc., the common rule for balancing is that the harder/riskier something is to do, the more the player should be rewarded for pulling it off (Figure 3.12). As an example, many fighting games feature a type of character known as a grappler. Grapplers often have a harder time reaching the opposing character and can't perform long-range attacks, and require more advanced input commands for their attacks. To balance this, grapplers will do far more damage compared to other character types, and one good hit can often turn an entire match around.

In soulslikes, the different defensive options highlight this kind of balance. Blocking has the least risk and the least reward for doing it, but parrying an attack (if it's possible) not only stops all damage but lets the player do even more damage when following up. There are plenty of examples of bosses in soulslikes and action games where being able to parry their moves completely shuts down the boss's ability to do anything to the player.

As I said in the last section, as the designer, you are not required to have a fixed set of offensive and defensive options in your game, but you need to make sure

3. The Basics of Action Design

that you are providing the players with everything they need to be able to win. Explaining all this will come down to onboarding and building a good tutorial. How most soulslikes will do this is through their opening areas and the world design; topics that I will return to in Chapter 8. There is so much more to action design and creating a combat system that is beyond the scope of this book, and when I do a Deep Dive on the genre itself, these topics will return there.

4

Foundations of RPG Design

4.1 What Is Abstracted Design?

It's time to turn to the other half of the equation that makes up soulslike design. Abstracted design or RPG gameplay is about the characters and their attributes determining the success of the game, and less on the player's reflexes (Figure 4.1). If you would like a larger look at the history of the RPG genre and many of its various subgenres, you can find that in *Game Design Deep Dive: Role Playing Games*.

For this book, the main area of abstracted design that soulslike designers make use of comes from progression and increasing the power of the player's character. In reflex-driven games, progression is focused on the player getting better at the game: Memorizing attack patterns, learning the muscle memory for combat, improving their reflexes and ability to quickly react, and so on. As I said further up, it's that reason why action games have a high-skill floor and can lead to a lot of player churn. Abstracted progression is about the in-game character, or the player's **avatar**, growing in power – allowing them to take more damage, hit harder, perform more attacks etc. In effect, the player's own reflexes and skills in the game are oftentimes secondary to being able to improve their character and give them more power. With that said, there are plenty of soulslike fans who have

DOI: 10.1201/9781003450078-4

Figure 4.1

Abstracted design has become incredibly popular as a way of adding more depth and longevity to games, and a mainstay of live service titles. It can be in everything from dungeon crawlers like the *Etrian Odyssey* series (re-released in 2023 by Atlus) on the left, to tactical strategy like *XCOM 2* (released in 2016 by Firaxis) on the right.

done no hit challenges or those where they only stay at level 1 and do not upgrade their characters. I'll talk more about the act of leveling in the next section.

Being able to upgrade the weapons and equipment that a character uses is another form of progression. Not every soulslike lets the player upgrade everything, but most these days at least allow them to upgrade their weapons and armor – allowing them to do more damage or take it respectively. Being able to upgrade gear also has the side effect of letting the player continue using a specific weapon they like instead of having to constantly swap to something new. This is important for soulslike design and how weapons are designed differently which I will discuss in Section 6.3.

Progression is also built into the world of design itself. As a player gets further into the game or moves further from the opening areas, enemies will have their attributes scaled higher to compensate. The common enemy in the very first area will be far weaker compared to the common enemy near the end of the game.

In reflex-driven games, combat and the player's ability are as close to 1:1 as possible – if the player's character does an uppercut that hits very hard, there are no calculations that need to be done to prove how hard it hits. In abstracted design, a lot happens between the character hitting an enemy, and that enemy receiving damage (Figure 4.2). Attributes like the property of the attack, the defense of the enemy, and even the character's skill at using said weapon, will

Figure 4.2

The difference between a game that focuses on abstracted design vs. reflex-driven design is how much the attributes of the character will factor into success or not. In *Fallout 4* pictured here (released in 2015 by Bethesda Game Studio), even though this looks like a scene out of a first-person shooter, all results in combat are based on character attributes more so than just having good reflexes.

dictate the actual damage done. In video games that were built off tabletop or pen and paper games, the rules and logic behind the scenes were the judge of how any damage was done. Even if the player can shoot an enemy directly in the head with a gun, if their character was rated poor for guns, that bullet may hardly do any damage compared to a punch to the face.

What's important to remember about abstracted progression for soulslike design, is that it provides a buffer and alternative if the player's reflexes aren't good enough to get past a fight. A major aspect of how soulslikes were more approachable compared to traditional action games is that as the player, if you get stuck in an action game, there are no alternative solutions or things to do other than getting better. In a soulslike and thanks to abstracted progression, if someone gets stuck at a hard fight, they can go upgrade their equipment, level up to get more health, or even rebuild their character around a different way of playing. The number of ways that a game can make use of abstract design is vast, and why there are so many subgenres of RPG design. For this book, I'm going to only be focusing on the ones that pertain to a soulslike design.

4.2 Learning Leveling

In the last section I talked about progression, and it's time to discuss what that means in its basic form with leveling. The act of leveling is something that has

Figure 4.3

Leveling up a character is the most direct way of having abstracted progression. In *Dark Souls 1* pictured here, you can see what my attributes are which reflect what kind of character I'm building and the gear I can use efficiently.

existed in every RPG in some aspect since the beginning of the genre. From an abstract perspective, it is supposed to measure a character becoming more skilled and better trained in their world. For the player, it provides an easy-to-understand metric for the overall strength of a character. The higher the level, the more powerful or dangerous that character is (Figure 4.3). A lot of modern games that use RPG systems will also tie a level directly to the progression of the game – limiting where the player can go or what options they have available based on the level of their character. This can be achieved implicitly by having stronger enemies whose stats are far greater than the player's character at the start, or explicitly by stating that the player cannot access areas until their level meets the threshold.

The act and requirements for leveling up differ based on the RPG itself, but for soulslikes, they use the most common action of defeating enemies to gain experience. In the next chapter, I'll talk about how From Software tweaked their earning experience with their games.

By leveling up, the player can increase the attributes of their character; making them stronger or giving them the ability to use different gear and weapons. Soulslikes can have either an implicit or explicit way to gate what gear a player can use. Some games specifically tell the player that to use a specific spell or wield a weapon properly, their stats must be at certain thresholds. A more flexible alternative is that the player can use every weapon or spell in the game, but said options receive a boost based on the character's stats. This is also referenced as scaling and here is an example:

Combat Knife

- Type: Knife
- Damage Type: Slashing
- Base Damage: 30
- Weapon Size: 1 Handed
- Attribute Scaling: Dexterity B–, Strength D+

In this example, if the player was building a character that was dexterity-focused, the knife would receive increased damage based on how high the attribute is. They would also receive a benefit from increasing their strength, however, it would be a far smaller boost per each point. Depending on the soulslike, attribute scaling can either be very important to boosting weapons for the main game or be something that only matters if the player has reached the end of the game and has their stats very high.

Being able to manually adjust what attributes get increased each level has become standard practice for soulslikes, as the genre is heavily built on the player being able to choose what kind of character to create and play. There isn't a hard list of what attributes must be featured in the game, but here are some basic ones that you can start with:

- Vitality: An attribute that raises the character's health
- Strength: Affects the damage the character does with melee weapons
- Intelligence: Affects the strength of magical attacks
- Endurance: Affects the amount of stamina a character has and their weight limit (if applicable)

This is just a simple list, and the names of each attribute aren't as important as what they do. Some soulslikes will give each attribute several areas that it will impact, with carryover between some attributes. For endurance, in games where there is a weight limit for how much a character can wear, this attribute would also increase the maximum weight for each point.

Depending on the design, there might be both a hard and soft cap on how leveling will impact a character. A hard cap means there is a literal end point to how high a character can level or how high their attributes can go. A soft cap is when an attribute hits a point when adding more to it will not impact the character; indicating to the player that they should level up something else.

Like all the other topics in this chapter, there is far more about the act and balancing of leveling not related to soulslike design, and again, my book on RPG design goes into more detail about them.

4.3 Basic Balancing

Balancing abstracted design is a huge topic, and that chapter of my book on RPGs was the longest in it. For the reader, RPG balancing comes down to both the numbers at play and something more abstract – the overall utility that a choice provides.

I've spoken at length in previous books and design posts about how tricky the balance is with abstracted design. For soulslikes that combine it with reflex-driven gameplay, it means that every choice needs to be weighted based on its stats and how it feels for the player to control it.

As the section header states, this is going to focus on the absolute basic philosophies that go with abstracted design. When looking at the utility and raw numbers of any skill or abstracted piece of gear, you want the "weight" of that option to reflect how safe or dangerous it is to use or reflected in the overall utility (Figure 4.4). The riskier something is to pull off in a game, the more reward there should be to do that. If someone requires far more resources to be spent to do it, then that should be reflected in the impact that option has. This can be seen in the difference between using small weapons vs. large ones, a stronger healing spell vs. a weaker one, having to charge an attack for an extra turn, and many other examples.

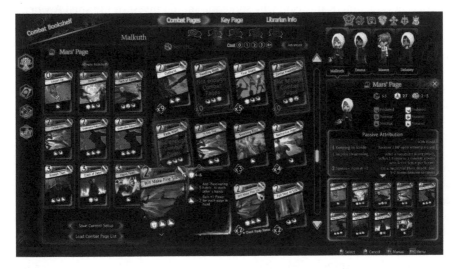

Figure 4.4

The deck builder genre is a good one to study how different elements can be factored together to try and create a form of balance. In *Library of Ruina* pictured here (released in 2021 by Project Moon), cards are balanced based on their overall cost and where they show up in the game. The further in, the more powerful and unique cards become, with power a deciding factor for how much that card costs to use.

If you want something to be viable in your game, there must be a reason to use it that reflects the risk of doing it. This is why fast weapons are often the lowest in terms of raw damage because the player can use them quickly, avoid a counter hit, and can more easily move around their opponent. Conversely, heavy two-handed weapons should always have higher damage values – if someone can pull off a hit with a weapon that is slow, highly telegraphed, and leave them wide open while attacking, then that hit should be incredibly high. However, many RPGs will obscure these numbers with other attributes, and this is how these games can become very complicated to play.

Those fast weapons I mentioned above. Now, let's picture they have a modifier that gives them a greater chance of scoring a critical hit, or one that does incredibly high damage. In this scenario, it is possible for a faster and lower damaging weapon to do more damage per second (or DPS) compared to a heavier weapon that is stronger.

Regarding spells, you want the cost of the spell to correlate to the utility that spell has. If we have two spells –

Spell A: Costs 10 MP, heals one party member for 20 points of health.
Spell B: Costs 8 MP, heals the entire party to full health and increases the damage done for 5 turns.

There is never a practical reason why someone should invest or use spell A when spell B does everything and more at a lower cost. It is possible to create additional conditionals or elements that can factor in, such as how long it takes to cast it, but you want to avoid having spells or options that serve no use within your game.

In any abstract design, creating specific builds, or playstyles, is one of the most rewarding aspects and what drives people to play these games besides the story. Discussing this layer of RPG design is out of scope for this book and especially for this section, and you'll find a huge discussion of this in *Game Design Deep Dive: Role Playing Games*.

Creating perfect balance in any game with different abilities, items, etc., is fundamentally impossible. If you have a spellcaster whose whole build is about shooting ice beams at enemies, and someone who fights with swords, both players are not going to have a 1:1 experience (Figure 4.5). The goal is that every build, every skill, and so on, should be viable throughout your game. Some parts should be obviously easier, some harder, but there should never be an encounter or enemy design that flat out rejects a certain playstyle. Even if you do allow the player to redo, or **respec**, their character, completely rebuilding a character is something that should only be done as a last resort, not for every fight.

As soulslikes evolved, so did the number of ways of playing them. You need to make sure that every build has the tools and options at their disposal to win, and this was one of the major shakeups that occurred as the genre evolved over the 2010s.

Figure 4.5

Builds in soulslikes can be powerful, weird, completely impractical, completely game-breaking, and anything else you want. Your role as the designer is to make sure that people understand what you expect out of the player to win and provide them with the means of doing so. There will always be people who will use the most outlandish builds possible, but you at least need to set a baseline of what's required to win.

5

How From Software
Defined Soulslikes

5.1 The Big Bang of Soulslikes with *Demon's Souls*

An alternate title to this book could be "How From Software Conquered the Game Industry" as the company was mainly known for small to modest successes for more than a decade. The story of how *Demon's Souls* became a worldwide phenomenon is an interesting one. The game's design came from Hidetaka Miyazaki who has become a household name for fans of the series and soulslikes (Figure 5.1).

During the 2000s, From Software continued to make games that were moderately successful and attracted a cult fanbase; thanks to continuing the *Armored Core* franchise and their different first-person RPGs I discussed in Chapter 2. In 2008, the game was first revealed at the Tokyo Gaming Show to huge negative feedback due to its difficulty. Sony, who published the Japanese version, didn't want to take a risk on the game outside of Japan and refused to publish international versions of it. Instead, for the only time to date for From Software, their game was published internationally by Atlus's Western publishing division.

When the game was released, reviews were across the board, primarily because of the difficulty, and this will be a point that I'll be focusing on in Chapter 7. The

DOI: 10.1201/9781003450078-5

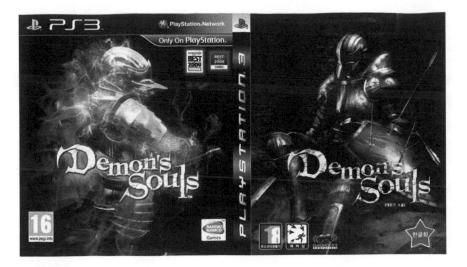

Figure 5.1

Here are the US and Japanese box arts for the game that would change From Software as a studio forever and launch the entire subgenre of this book. Note: the art on the left is updated after the initial release and does not reflect Atlus as the original US publisher.

one thing everyone who played the game agreed on was that this was a very different game compared to anything else on the market.

It's important to remember that the 2000s was a period when game design began to become standardized among the major platforms. With gamepads 100% fixed in terms of basic layout and functionality, it meant it was possible to create the same gameplay experience on an Xbox just as on a PlayStation. The one outlier was Nintendo with the Wii and Wii-U platforms. For game design itself, this was a period where the industry began to see **AAA** games start to homogenize around several gameplay principles and designs. In part, this was one of the reasons that led to the horror genre dying out in the late 2000s into the 2010s on the major platforms, with studios focusing on multiplayer and shooters (Figure 5.2).

At the start of the 2000s, this was when some of the most challenging action and reflex-driven games were released – with many of them being so difficult that it became a badge of honor to finish them. However, this also meant that the audience for these games were noticeably smaller, and there were more discussions throughout the 2000s about trying to make games that everyone could beat. It's funny to think about it now, writing this in 2023, with so many challenging games released over the 2010s, but *Demon's Souls* was a turning point that even with *Elden Ring's* success in 2022, a lot of people hadn't really processed why. I'll discuss this further at the end of this chapter.

I'll be focusing on *Dark Souls* in the next section, and while it did become the blueprint for this subgenre, *Demon's Souls'* structure is the one that started it all.

Figure 5.2

The AAA game industry by the end of the 2000s became focused on multiplayer experience and the burgeoning live service industry. Games like *League of Legends* and *Team Fortress 2* (released in 2009 by Riot Games and 2007 by Valve, respectively), were two of the most popular games for their multiplayer experiences.

The story was that the player had come to the land of Boletaria in search of finding a way to defeat a curse that had enveloped the land. From the tutorial itself, *Demon's Souls* distinguished itself from other games by ending it with a boss that would be able to kill the player in one hit. For everyone starting the game for the first time, this fight would end with them dying, although it was possible to beat it during the tutorial. From there, players are taken to the hub area known as the Nexus. Their goal is to explore the various areas of the kingdom to defeat the strongest monsters, or demons, to gather their souls to gain access to King Allant who is the perpetrator of the curse and the one standing in the player's way of ending it. Each one of the game's five "worlds" is broken down into different stages. While the player can start any world in any order, they must go through each one of its stages in order from first to last (Figure 5.3).

The differences in how *Demon's Souls* was played extended from the gameplay to its unique systems and rules. By far the most iconic is how death and experience are handled. Defeating enemies grants the player their souls which act as the game's currency and experience – the stronger the enemy, the more souls they are worth. If the player is defeated, all accumulated souls are dropped at the point where they die. On each death or reload of a stage, all enemies are revived and returned to their established positions. If the player is killed before getting their souls back, that total is lost forever. There is no way to "bank" souls – the player must either spend them at vendors, upgrade their gear with them, or use them to raise their level and attributes. There were consumable items that were worth a

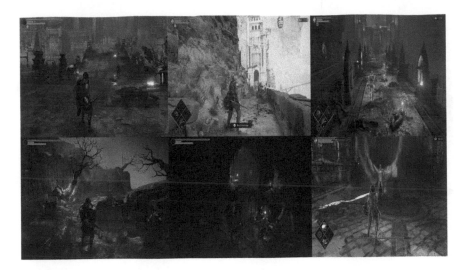

Figure 5.3

Demon's Souls had the most straightforward path out of all the soulslikes. Each world featured a completely different setting with unique challenges, with the boss Old King Allant who could only be reached once worlds 2–5 were finished.

fixed number of souls the player could hoard, but this was a limited option. This would cement the act of tension as a major part of the soulslike genre: that even if the player just defeated a tough enemy or survived a hard fight, if they can't get back to safety and use those souls, there is always the risk that they could lose them forever.

The game's multiplayer was another concept that no one else had done before. While the game itself was a single-player experience, it was possible for other players to enter each other's game to help or hurt the host player. This was tied to the two states a character could be in human form and soul form. While in human form, a character has access to their full health bar and can summon players in soul form to help them out. Other players in soul form could invade a human character's game to kill them and take their souls. When a character in human form dies, they return in soul form – having access to only half their maximum health without the use of a specific ring. While in soul form, they are once again able to be summoned or invade another game. To return to human form, the player must either defeat a boss in their game, use a limited available item, or help another player defeat a boss.

While future soulslikes by From Software would keep the multiplayer concept, one system that hasn't been seen since *Demon's Souls* was "world tendency." Each time a player in human form is killed in one of the game's five worlds, the world tendency of that area would shift closer to black; conversely, killing a boss or other specific characters would shift it toward white. A white tendency world would reduce the attributes of enemies and make it easier to play. A black

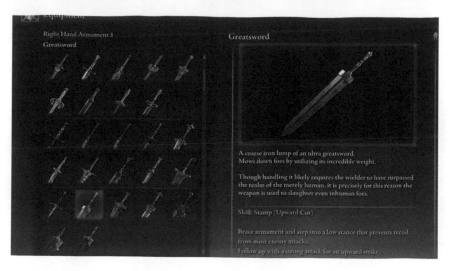

Figure 5.4

Item descriptions throughout all From Software's soulslike games always came with more than just what the item did. This became an effective lore device to flesh out the world and give more personality to bosses that would drop specific rewards.

tendency world made the enemies harder and would open specific areas where players could find harder enemies for unique rewards. While the system was interesting and different, it did present one major design problem. Because dying triggered the world tendency change, it meant that players who were constantly dying while using human form were making the game harder for themselves without realizing it. Part of good game design and good difficulty design is that you do not want to punish players who are having trouble with your game by making it harder. Following *Demon's Souls*, the world tendency system has not been seen in any form in future titles.

Another social system that was first featured here was the use of messaging and death markers. Players could leave messages everywhere in the game using a combination of preset words. This was used to help players, lie to them about upcoming dangers, or just say something completely random about the situation. When a character is killed, a blood stain is left on the ground so that other players can view the last 5 seconds of a character's life before they are killed; providing them with intel about what is going on in this area.

The storytelling that *Demon's Souls* introduced would also become another staple not only of From Software, but of future soulslikes (Figure 5.4). Instead of relying heavily on narration and story, *Demon's Souls* paints a very vivid picture of the world using lore that the player can find on every weapon, item, and piece of gear in the game. Defeat a boss, and you can learn more about them if you choose by viewing the item description on their soul. The actual plot and history that takes place in any of From Software's games is quite vast, but the game never stops to explain to the player what is going on and leaves it up to them to discover it. There are people who have made multi-hour examinations of the lore of each game.

As I discussed in the previous chapter, being able to upgrade the attributes of a character was one of the major forms of progression, but there was one other way for players to improve their chances at survival. It was possible to upgrade weapon levels using specific resources. At specific thresholds, players would need to find higher-quality resources to continue upgrading that specific weapon. It was also possible to transform a weapon's properties by using a specific resource per upgrade. These upgrades could not be combined with anything else and would allow players to tweak their gear to match a specific playstyle.

The different weapons and ways of building characters were also distinct from other games and would define From Software's style throughout the decade. There were three broad ways of playing *Demon's Souls* – close combat with melee weapons, using spells, and using bows for long-ranged attacks. Every melee weapon had a different range, attack animation, and attack speed to master. Using a weapon that swung wide in a narrow corridor meant that it would bounce off walls and leave the character momentarily defenseless. The player could technically use any weapon regardless of the attribute requirements, but the weapon would do very little damage. The only exception was being able to hold a heavy weapon with two hands to compensate for not having the strength to wield it with just one. As I discussed in Chapter 3, players could block, dodge, or parry attacks. The shield that the player used would affect how much damage was blocked and the cost to the player's stamina. Run out of stamina while fighting, and it was not possible to attack or defend while the player waited for the stamina gauge to start refilling. *Demon's Souls* would also incentivize being stealthy via "backstab" attacks. If the character attacks an enemy directly in their back, it would trigger a backstab – causing far more damage and knocking the enemy down.

Spell use has always been an interesting aspect of the soulslikes. In *Demon's Souls*, spell use was tied to magic power, like with the character's health, which could be restored by using a consumable item. Spell utility greatly varied – from direct damage spells to those that could increase the character's attributes, situational spells, and much more. When I talk about the later games, they would have different ways and balancing for spells.

For range, this required the player to equip a bow and corresponding arrows. While the player could use the game's lock-on feature, it was also possible to go into a first-person perspective and free-aim arrows at enemies. The advantage of range was that it gave the player an option to engage with enemies without alerting the enemies around them or deliver damage safely before engaging in melee.

These different ways of playing would become more elaborate over the course of the entire soulslike franchise and provided different playstyles for fans to learn. There are people who use the same style from game to game, challenge themselves with unique builds, or ignore specific options. Despite the objection from hardcore fans, there is no one "right" way of playing a soulslike.

Besides everything mentioned here, *Demon's Souls* would also introduce everyone to a different kind of level and enemy design that I will talk more about in Chapter 8.

Demon's Souls would also begin a trend of providing reasons to replay each soulslike in different ways. Once someone beats the game, they can restart the game using their completed build, with all the enemies in the game having their stats scaled up to provide more challenge and allow the player to keep upgrading their character's attributes. This is also referred to as "new game plus." For the truly dedicated, there were multiple new game pluses, each one making the game even more difficult for players who wanted that. Another reason to replay these games was for players who wanted to collect every piece of equipment in the game. Every boss soul could be used at specific vendors to create a unique weapon or spell related to it. However, once used, that soul was removed for the remainder of the playthrough. At a minimum, someone would have to replay the game twice to collect all the missing unlocks.

From a gameplay point of view, *Demon's Souls* is the most dated in terms of its soulslike design. Of all the entries by From Software, it is the slowest one to play. Earlier in this book, I mentioned how characters had different ways of dodging damage based on the weight of the character's equipment. *Demon's Souls* is the only one in the series that would take this a step further and would also count all the miscellaneous items, and spare weapons and equipment in the character's backpack, as part of the weight requirement. Later games would just count the active equipment as part of the character's weight. With that said, it also received a remake in 2020 to update the graphics and gameplay.

After everything was said and done, with all the turmoil and issues before release, *Demon's Souls* would go on to sell several hundred thousand copies during its initial release, with the exact number hard to locate. By comparison, the remake has sold over 1 million copies to date (Figure 5.5). Its success would also lead to a new partnership between From Software and the developer/publisher Bandai Namco, who would become their new global publisher and would publish most of their games, with the exception of a few others that I will talk about later in this chapter.

5.2 How *Dark Souls* Became the Soulslike Blueprint

There is a common theme in a lot of the genres in the game industry – that the first game to create or coin a new genre is often not the one that blows it up. Instead, that distinction will fall on the game that refines the concepts into becoming the staple of the genre. With soulslikes, that would go to From Software's second attempt with *Dark Souls* released in 2011 (Figure 5.6).

The story takes place in a world that is kept alive thanks to the powers of the "first flame." During the end of the second age of flame, people are becoming cursed by a mark known as a "darksign," With it, the person cannot be killed and will keep reviving, but this also will lead to that person going mad or "turn

Figure 5.5

Demon's Souls is the only soulslike by From Software now that has been fully remastered for the current generation of platforms, namely the PlayStation 5. And fans continue to wonder if there will be similar treatment with the *Dark Souls* series at some point.

Figure 5.6

Dark Souls's remastered edition was not a complete rebuild like the *Demon's Souls* one, and for the PC version at least, there to fix the problems with the original port.

hollow." As one such individual, the player finds their character locked up in an asylum for the undead before being let out to explore and either keep the flame going or put it out. From a storytelling standpoint, *Dark Souls* would begin another trend of this series with the player exploring a dead or dying world.

Like *Demon's Souls*, the game's opening features a fight with a very tough enemy before the player is allowed to reach the hub area and begin exploring in full. While the basic gameplay remains the same, several redesigns and additions would cement *Dark Souls* as the standard of soulslikes for the decade. The first big change came in the form of the estus flask. Instead of having to buy healing items that were consumed upon use, going forward, each game would give the player a replenishable healing item. The estus flask could be upgraded by finding specific items in the world to make it more potent and increase the number of uses. When the flask runs out, the only way to restore it is to return to *Dark Souls'* new checkpointing system – bonfires. Throughout the world, the player can find bonfires that act as safe havens and areas where their character can respawn if they are killed. Using a bonfire is also where they can level up their character, but any use will revive all defeated enemies in the area.

It's hard to really explain to someone new to design why the estus flask was a huge deal for soulslikes and game design philosophy. The problem that RPGs and action games have had since their inception was making the character's health an essential resource to manage, but still providing the player with the means of regaining it. Many games have consumable healing items, including *Demon's Souls*, that once the player runs out, there is no way of regaining them within the level itself; forcing the player to stop what they're doing and replenish their reserves. In games where healing could only be done by finding items within the level, it meant there was a fixed amount of health a player could recover. Action games in the 2000s started to use regenerating health – where the player would have to hide for a minute or two to regain their health (Figure 5.7). The problem with it was that it slowed the pacing of the game down and took the player out of the gameplay to do it. By giving every player a replenishable method, it turned the act of healing into its own mechanic and risk/reward element. Drinking from the flask leaves the player momentarily defenseless and requires the player to find a safe window during combat to do it. Instead of punishing players long-term for using up their healing, it only impacts players in the short-term – players still had to properly manage their healing and the damage they were taking, but now, they knew that they could get their healing back very easily.

Instead of having the game set up as a series of stages, this is the game that would popularize having a quasi-open world structure. Each major area in the game is its own biome of content – with specific enemies, items, and hazards to get through. Again, I'll discuss the unique level design in more detail in Chapter 8. Each area connects to one or more other areas in the world, with many roads leading back to the game's hub. The only exceptions are the areas connecting from the region known as "Anor Londo," which reaches it marks about the half-way point through the main quest of the game. Clearing Anor Londo unlocks

Figure 5.7

Regenerating health first began to be integrated into action games with the *Halo* series in the 2000s originally developed by Bungie, and following it, most action-based games switched to it in lieu of having recovery items in the levels. There would not be a shakeup in this kind of design until the appearance of the estus flask in *Dark Souls*, and then the evolution of push-forward combat in the 2010s.

the back half of challenges and the ability to teleport to specific bonfires using a specific item. This kind of movement is often referred to as "fast travel" and is a major feature in any game that has a huge game space to explore.

Dark Souls would continue the player having two states of their character as either human or hollow. This did not affect the attributes of a character but did impact specific quests and gear the player could use. The ability to summon other players or be invaded by them continued here.

The use of spells was also changed to make them harder to use as the only form of attack. Instead of the character having a resource to use spells, every spell had a specific number of charges the player could use during combat. Run out, and that spell would become unavailable until they recharge at a bonfire. The number of spells that a character could have active at one time was also dependent on the "attunement" attribute. Spells in all the games have vastly different effects, some were built around specific types of damage, and others were meant to be supportive and help the player in other ways besides attacking.

Melee combat was sped up compared to *Demon's Souls*, and the game featured far more weapons, shields, and armor to use. Most noticeably, allowing players to upgrade individual armor pieces to provide more defense, as well as upgrade shields so that they could block more damage effectively.

Dark Souls would also open another aspect of the gameplay in the form of player vs. player or PVP content. The act of invading someone's game to fight

Figure 5.8

From Software has a habit in their games that the back half challenges are often more frustrating than the first half. *The Bed of Chaos* boss fight on the left is considered one of the worst bosses in the series due to its frustrating design and requiring a jump to get past it. The crystal cave features invisible paths that the player must figure out how to navigate or fall to their death.

them has been an established element in each title. However, starting with *Dark Souls* there was more attention put on the balancing and act of fighting each other. Spells and weapons started to have different effects based on fighting other enemies or fighting other players. With *Dark Souls*, this would be the first, but not the last game, to have an area 100% exclusive for PVP. Often taking the form of an arena, it's a place where anyone who wants to fight other players could go to challenge each other. As it turns out, offering many ways of building characters and going through the game also lent itself well to fighting other players and really making use of all those different play styles.

The success of *Dark Souls* catapulted From Software's renown even further and is considered one of the best games released in the 2010s across all platforms. Finding exact sales numbers was hard but estimates around the internet for the number of copies sold of *Dark Souls 1* being around 10 million, and I will talk about the other entries in the next section.

As I titled this section, *Dark Souls* and the entire series became the defining benchmark for soulslikes. From a design point of view, *Dark Souls* does hold up better than *Demon's Souls* but does feel restrictive in terms of gameplay compared to later entries and later soulslikes. It would be a very long time before movement would evolve in these games, and it did introduce some negative tropes to the series (Figure 5.8). The back half of the game is not looked at as memorable as the first, with some of the series' most annoying and frustrating areas to explore.

5. How From Software Defined Soulslikes

Part of the problem was that the original version of the game and the PC port had noticeable issues when it came to rendering specific environments and had massive framerate loss causing the game to hitch during play. These issues would be improved when the game was re-released in 2018. A running joke of the series is that each game features one very difficult area to explore that often has poison in it, and the *Dark Souls'* area was "Blight town." A faintly lit vertical area with multiple ways of falling to death, enemies that could cause poison by shooting blowdarts, and the entire floor of the area was one giant poison swamp. Still, this did not dissuade fans from playing and beating the game with all kinds of builds. The game received additional support in an expansion that added in a brand-new area, which would also mark a positive trend of each soulslike receiving more content to challenge players further.

5.3 The Rest of From Software's Successes

In each Deep Dive, I try to give a history of the respective genre, and this time, we have perhaps the shortest history to cover, as soulslikes have only existed for a little over a decade, with the ones by From Software considered the highest rated.

As with any popular genre or game, other developers will try to make their own mark both in the indie and AAA spaces, and soulslikes were no exception. To make things easier to follow, I'm going to focus on From Software's lineup first and then talk about the other studios that did their own takes in the next section. The reason why I'm spending so much time here to talk about From Software is that it is not hyperbole to say that the rest of the industry turned to them in terms of evolving the soulslike design; with each successful game further providing lessons that other designers took to heart with their takes.

With the success of *Dark Souls*, From Software would spend the rest of the decade working on entries and series that would take the soulslike design in different directions. *Dark Souls 2* was released in 2014 and fans remember this one the most as the one game that Miyazaki supervised but did not direct, as he was working on the next entry in this section (Figure 5.9). *Dark Souls 2* featured more weapon variety compared to the previous game, along with more advanced enemy designs. It was possible to equip two weapons of the same type and make use of specific dual-wielding combo attacks with them. Unlike the first game, players were able to fast travel to the bonfires they had activated from the beginning. The level design and general game space were also bigger and more elaborate compared to the first game.

However, there were a few more pain points and polarizing mechanics in this game. The difficulty was across the board harder than the first game – featuring more pits to fall into, more and stronger enemies to fight, and the opening areas escalated the difficulty faster than other entries. Enemy designs became more advanced and would begin a trend of evolving the different attack patterns that I will discuss more in Section 8.2. One of the most controversial changes was how the I-frame on dodging was altered. In every other soulslike, the amount of

Figure 5.9

Dark Souls 2 represents the series going forward and trying to grow. It is larger and more advanced than the first, but also shows that if there are any issues with the base systems, it can hurt a game, and why it was rebalanced and re-released.

I-frame that occurs during a dodge is fixed. In this game, it was possible to raise a character's agility via the "adaptability" attribute. The higher a character's agility was, the more I-frames they would have during a dodge to a fixed amount. In any reflex-driven game, the more I-frames associated with an animation, the easier it was to perform dodges to avoid damage. According to unofficial fan guides, the number of I-frames could triple going from low agility to where it would cap. For players who tried to build a character focusing on melee attacks and dodging, it was all but required to focus on adaptability at the start of the game above any other attribute to get it taken care of as fast as possible.

Dark Souls 2 did have some high notes, it has some of the most varied locations and set pieces in the series, once again all connected throughout the game space. One area was a giant pirate cove complete with a ship the player had to board to fight the boss. The infamous "iron keep" was a castle floating in a giant pool of lava where players had to fight one of the hardest enemies for a first-time play – the smelter demon.

Even though *Dark Souls 2* was considered by many to be the weakest of the trilogy, fans would still agree that even a "lesser" From Software soulslike was still one of the best and highest-rated games of that year. In 2015, a revised edition of the game was released with the subtitle "Scholar of the First Sin," that revised enemy placements, reworked the online play, and was designed to be the definitive edition of the game, and was packaged with the additional **DLC** content that was sold separately in the base version.

5. How From Software Defined Soulslikes

Figure 5.10

Bloodborne stood out in a lot of ways from the *Dark Souls* trilogy, and the atmosphere certainly helped, with far more monster-type enemies to fight, and a completely different aesthetic and architecture.

As I said in the earlier section, Miyazaki during this time was working on another project by From Software, which would turn into a fan favorite and my personal favorite soulslike of the decade – *Bloodborne* (Figure 5.10). Released in 2015, it is the only game by From Software during this decade that was platform exclusive, being on the PlayStation 4. While the game drew obvious comparisons design-wise to the other soulslikes, it featured some subtle, and not-so-subtle, differences in the story and design. Taking place in the land known as Yharnam, players create a hunter who must explore the plague-ridden streets and countryside fighting people who have been transformed into monsters. A lot of the enemies and area designs evoke a Lovecraftian aesthetic as opposed to the medieval fantasy that the *Dark Souls* series was known for.

Combat was designed to be faster-paced and more offensive-focused compared to other soulslikes. Players could not block any attacks and instead had to rely on a dodge that was noticeably faster to perform compared to the dodge rolling in the *Dark Souls* trilogy. When the player's character takes damage, there is a small window where it is possible to recover that health by hitting enemies. Instead of focusing on a wide variety of weapons, *Bloodborne* has the shortest weapon list out of all From Software's soulslike. The weapons, or as they were called: "trick weapons," were designed to operate in two different modes. The threaded cane, one of three starter weapons in the game, was a cane that could transform into a whip while fighting. Besides each mode having its own feel and way of fighting with it, a player could transform their weapon in the middle of attacking for a transitionary attack, to then continue using the other mode.

Parrying was no longer done by using a defensive equipment; instead, every character could equip a gun that hitting the enemy with a bullet while they were attacking would momentarily stun them, and set them up for a "visceral attack" which was *Bloodborne's* version of the heavy attack. Instead of having different ways of playing and building a character, it was all about what trick weapon the player wanted to use. While there was an "arcane" attribute, this was for using some of the stranger weapons in the game, and there were no spells to find in it. This led to *Bloodborne's* combat being the most aggressively close-ranged out of all their soulslikes.

There are three aspects of *Bloodborne* that were unique to it that From Software at the time of writing this book have not repeated since. Unlike the *Dark Souls* games that had replenishable healing via the estus flasks, *Bloodborne* did not do that. Bullets and blood vials were consumables that had to be bought at the game's hub area. As someone progressed, the cost of buying both would go up to reflect the harder enemies that they were fighting. I am personally not a fan of this decision and consider it to be the one design complaint I have with *Bloodborne*. The reason is that the player cannot just hold an infinite number of both items, so it did not make sense to punish lesser-skilled players by having them spend more money to acquire these items compared to those who didn't need to use as many.

Besides upgrading weapons, players were able to find and attach gems to their weapons that would affect its attributes. Better gems would have more and stronger effects, and they were also randomly generated as rewards that could be found in the next example.

The next difference is that *Bloodborne* features procedurally generated content in the form of chalice dungeons. A chalice dungeon involved the player using a chalice, which affected the conditions and difficulty of the dungeon, to generate an area for the player to explore. Reaching the end of a dungeon would often reward the player with gems and a new chalice to make a harder dungeon.

The greater focus on combat and the variety of enemy designs and locations helped to cement *Bloodborne* as a fantastic game. In terms of difficulty, it is on the harder side, especially starting out, compared to From Software's other games. The differences in the combat system and how weapons worked, were put to the test very early in. One of the most recognizable bosses in the game, both for its theme and design, was Father Gascoigne (Figure 5.11). This was a fight that started out battling Gascoigne while he was human, to then have him transform into a beast halfway through, adopting a completely different move set and attack pattern. The game would repeat this trend with another fan-favorite boss fight, this time in the DLC with Ludwig who again, went through two completely different phases for how they fought.

Despite only being available on the PlayStation 4, the game has still sold more than 2 million copies, but it is still hard to find official sales for these games. It is also the game that fans have requested the most to be ported to other platforms, but there is no news as of writing this book about a port coming.

5. How From Software Defined Soulslikes

Figure 5.11

The first boss of a soulslike is the metric that many fans will use to judge the quality of the game, as this is where the first big test of the game comes from. Father Gascoigne is remembered as a fantastic boss who tests the player's knowledge of the game to be aggressive but still pays attention. His transformation is also a major shock as the first boss of these games typically doesn't transform like this during their fight.

In 2016, From Software released what would become the final game in the *Dark Souls* trilogy with #3. *Dark Souls 3* removed the ability for players to improve their I-frames and reduced the weapon variety in one respect but introduced something else to replace it in the form of weapon skills. Every weapon and shield in the game came with a respective "skill," this could be something as generic as being able to parry attacks, to one-off skills unique to specific pieces of gear. The concept was that besides the player customizing their character based on their playstyle, the different weapon skills would allow someone to further define how they played the game. The option to dual-wield any weapon was replaced by weapons that were just two copies of the same weapon counting as one.

In terms of design, *Dark Souls 3* would strike a balance between allowing people to play the game purely as spellcasters, while still providing limitations for the playstyle. Players still had a limit on the number of spells they could equip at one time, but restricting the use of each individual spell was removed. In its place, players were given a second kind of estus flask in the form of the "ashen estus flask." Instead of restoring health, the ashen flask would restore magic power – allowing someone to keep using spells provided they had enough power. To compensate, players could decide how much of the overall number of times they could use a flask that was dedicated to either the healing or magic restoring

Figure 5.12

The trilogy ended on a high note with *Dark Souls 3*, featuring a lot of interesting boss fights like the ones in this shot. While it didn't do as many things differently compared to #2 or is as famous as #1, it still rounds out the trilogy and cements the *Dark Souls* franchise as the best soulslikes of the 2010s.

one. For players who focused on melee builds, they could completely ignore the ashen flask in favor of having more heals during combat.

Like the other games in the series, *Dark Souls 3* was considered one of the best games of the year, received two DLC episodes, and at this time, is the final game in the *Dark Souls* series (Figure 5.12).

With that said, there was one other game developed by From Software released during the decade with *Sekiro: Shadows Die Twice* in 2019. While the game borrowed several major conventions of soulslike design, I would not label it as a soulslike like the other games mentioned in this section and chapter. In the next chapter, I will go into more detail about the specific mechanics and systems that make up soulslike design.

As for *Sekiro*, the focus of the gameplay was a parry combat system. By hitting the block button at the right time, the player could parry incoming attacks, and this was done to affect the enemy's "posture" meter. When the posture meter completely fills up, the player is allowed to perform a finishing move on the opponent – killing them instantly if they were not considered a boss. For boss fights, each one had multiple health bars that represented phases of the fight. When the boss's health empties out, either from posture breaking or just damage, the boss would move into their next phase, changing their attack pattern accordingly. If the player doesn't time their blocks right, then it would affect their posture meter, and becoming stunned during a fight was almost certain death.

5. How From Software Defined Soulslikes

Figure 5.13

From Software is one of the few developers who come to mind who will cap off their tutorials with boss fights. *Dark Souls 2's* last giant pictured in the middle was at the end of the first major area. While the Asylum Demon and Ludux Gundyr bosses were a way of testing players to see if they could handle the rest of the game.

This kind of system would also go on to be seen in another action game that had similar elements of soulslike and roguelike design with *Sifu* (released in 2022 by Sloclap). *Sekiro*, like all From Software's games this decade, was praised for its challenging gameplay, but at the same time, did have critics who found these titles to be too difficult to play. I'll be focusing on difficulty design in Chapter 7, as there is a lot to go over.

For the entirety of the 2010s, From Software's name and recognition continued to grow and will easily be remembered as one of the best decades for the studio. There are some interesting lessons on game design that we can learn from this period. Having a specific focus or intent for your gameplay and design is important if you want to capture a certain market. From Software's games have always been on the niche side; even when we talk about the successes of *Armored Core, Dark Souls,* and *Elden Ring.* Part of the success of the 2010s was not only the market catching up to them – with consumers wanting more challenging games, but also a willingness to focus on making the gameplay as attractive to play as possible. There are hundreds of unique and challenging games released on the PC in the 90s; designs that have never been copied or updated since with hardened fanbases. However, these games feature incredibly dated UIs, are hard to learn, and do very little to invite someone to try and play them. While *Demon's Souls,* and the *Dark Souls* series, did have some confusing UIs, the core gameplay loop was easy to grasp, and the developers kept improving the onboarding and early area designs as the series went on (Figure 5.13).

As I'll talk about in Chapter 7 with difficulty, part of the subtle brilliance of From Software's design and approach to challenge has been their approach to challenge and progression. Each game I mentioned in this section is by no means an easy game to play, but conversely, they're not very hard to learn. The player is given enough tools, items, and ways of playing, to allow someone who "gets it" to be able to win. So much of the difficulty of these games came down to a lack of knowledge of how to play them. For every single person who picked up one of these games, I can guarantee that their first-ever playthrough had them dying at least 50 times. Once someone gets the muscle memory down and understands the game, a lot of the difficulty goes away. There are people who have done no-hit challenges in all the games, even some who have beaten the games without leveling up their character.

5.4 The *Dark Souls* of Everything Else

I've said this line before in previous Deep Dives: when a game achieves massive success, other developers will soon follow suit with their own takes to try and strike while the iron is hot. Even though From Software had hit after hit with their soulslikes, there were numerous attempts by smaller studios and indie developers to make their own. An interesting point, and why it's going to be hard to catalog every game here, is that "soulslike" became the new buzz term to describe any difficult game. During the 2010s, a lot of studios rebranded their games as soulslikes or, "The *Dark Souls* of X" where X is any kind of genre. To keep things focused, I'm only going to be talking about games that attempted to convey the similar mechanics and design of a soulslike; so, I won't be covering the "*Dark Souls* of hopscotch."

Despite *Demon's Souls* and *Dark Souls* being released in 2009 and 2011, respectively, it did take some time before other studios attempted their own takes. The first major example was *Lords of the Fallen* released in 2014 by Deck 13. The game did well at the time as the first major game to evoke the soulslike design outside of From Software, but fans seem to agree that it doesn't hold up as well as the other games. The success did lead to Deck 13 continuing and refining their design with the more successful *The Surge* series (#1 released in 2017, #2 released in 2019) (Figure 5.14). To this day, *The Surge* games stand out for being one of the few soulslikes not to be set in a fantasy or medieval setting. Taking place in the future, players had to fight robots and humans in powerful exoskeletons to save the world. Besides finding new weapons, the player could fit their exoskeleton with the parts of their defeated enemies to create different strategies. As of writing this book, there is a modern remaster planned for *Lords of the Fallen*.

The middle of the 2010s saw many indie developers adopting the "*Dark Souls* of X" marketing strategy for their games hoping to hit it big. The most successful at this time was the 2016's *Salt and Sanctuary* by Ska Studios. It is also noticeable for being one of the few soulslikes to work in 2D instead of 3D, and I will discuss why there is this difficulty in Chapter 8. The player creates a character that gets

Figure 5.14

As with any genre, using a different aesthetic/setting can help differentiate you from your contemporaries, and *The Surge* did just that. While it lacked the polish and balance of the *Dark Souls* trilogy, it did play quite differently than the other soulslikes, for better and worse.

washed ashore on a mysterious island after their ship is wrecked by a monster. From there, they must explore and discover the root of all the evil that plagues the area. The game featured a variety of weapons and gear that players could build their characters around. Many weapons could be upgraded to a higher tier – improving its stats and adding new properties to it. Progression was laid out over a massive passive skill tree. Investing points would raise the character's attributes and was the prerequisite to equip higher tier gear.

The game also borrowed elements from **metroidvania** design in the form of brands. Finding them throughout the world would unlock a movement ability that would open more areas to the player and was required to keep making progress in the world. Sales-wise, it sold well enough to get a sequel in 2022 with *Salt and Sacrifice*, and it stands to this day as one of the most well-received soulslikes and indie games of the last decade (Figure 5.15). Just as *Dark Souls* would inspire developers to make 3D soulslikes, *Salt and Sacrifice*'s model of combining metroidvania and soulslike design would go on to be its own source of inspiration for indie studios. Series like *Death's Gambit* (released in 2018 by White Rabbit), *Vigil: The Longest Night* (released in 2020 by Glass Heart Games), and *Ender Lilies: Quietus of the Knights* (released in 2021 by Live Wire and Adglobe) to name a few, would be their own take on this kind of design.

The year 2017 would mark the release of the only series that has come the closest to competing with From Software in terms of success and praise with *Nioh* developed by Team Ninja. Very loosely based off the story of William Adams, an

Figure 5.15

While it may not look it, making a soulslike in 2D is harder than it sounds due to the limitations of 2D when it comes to combat and exploration. *Salt and Sanctuary* succeeded as the most popular example of evoking soulslike design in 2D, with the addition of the metroidvania upgrades.

Englishman who would become a samurai in Japan in the 1600s. While the game took place in the real world, it focused on a supernatural resource called Amrita, which had the power to turn people into demons and summon spirits and monsters. William arrives in Japan seeking a mysterious character who has stolen a guardian spirit from him. Once in Japan, he learned swordsmanship and various techniques from many historical figures during the period to fight yokai, which are spirits and monsters that are part of Japanese folklore. *Nioh* stood apart from other soulslikes by being far faster-paced in terms of combat, which harkens back to the studio's successful action series *Ninja Gaiden* in the 2000s. Of the souslikes that have been released, it is the most combat-intensive, even more so than From Software's entries (Figure 5.16). Players could use different weapons; each type had its own combo system and feel of fighting. William could move between light, medium, and heavy stances while fighting – affecting the strength of his attacks and the rate he would go through stamina or ki in this game. Every enemy had a ki gauge that could be reduced with successful attacks and would cause them to become stunned if they ran out during combat. For the player, running out of ki would often mean death during one of the game's many boss fights.

While the game had many of the same trappings as the Souls series, it did stand out in two different ways. Unlike other soulslikes that used fixed equipment, *Nioh* would procedurally generate equipment that belonged to each weapon and armor type. While the base attributes for a weapon were consistent, the higher the rarity

5. How From Software Defined Soulslikes

Figure 5.16

It's impossible for me to show you how different *Nioh* feels to play with screenshots compared to *Dark Souls*. No other studio has managed to create a soulslike where combat is this intensive, and why the series is far harder to play compared to *Dark Souls*.

rating, the more passive modifiers that piece of gear could have. This did come at the cost of making it harder and more confusing when it came to selecting useful equipment to use. Some modifiers were borderline useless, and other ones would be huge. Instead of a dodge roll, there was just a dodge that the player could perform. Depending on the weight of the equipment worn, it would impact the speed and distance the player could travel while being invincible to damage.

These elements were expanded on in the sequel released in 2021 which also increased the ways players could fight enemies and gave the various yokai more damaging powers. In the sequel, one of the most important mechanics to learn was how to perform a "burst counter." In the first game, enemies would produce a red aura before they would do an unblockable attack and the player's only option was to get out of the way. In the sequel, by performing a specific counter move, the player could stop the attack and punish the enemy if they timed it right. It was also possible to equip various yokai spirits that the player could use their attacks during combat. The sequel also continued to increase the difficulty of the game by making enemy attacks more complex and giving bosses the ability to power up for a few minutes enhancing their damage and combo patterns. The success of *Nioh* was a shot in the arm that revitalized Team Ninja as a premier action game studio and would lead them to work on a *Final Fantasy* spin-off called *Stranger in Paradise* in 2022 and release a follow-up franchise to *Nioh* with *Wo Long: Fallen Dynasty* in 2023 that focuses on the "Romance of the Three Kingdoms" story.

Figure 5.17

Remnant 2 came out while I was finishing writing this book and continued the gameplay presented in the first one. Like *Nioh* that came before it, *Remnant* stands out from the rest of the market with a completely different take on the formula.

While *Nioh* has been the most successful, there were other 3D soulslikes that were released in the back half of the 2010s. The *Darksiders* series made a name for itself with each game drawing from different genres and gameplay, and the third one released in 2018 borrowed from the soulslike genre developed by Gunfire Games. *Ashen*, released in 2018 by A44, focused more on exploring an open world with either another player or AI partner and was noticeably easier compared to other soulslikes.

The year 2019 saw several new franchises released that took advantage of the soulslike design. *Remnant: From the Ashes*, also by Gunfire Games was the first attempt at combining a third-person shooter with soulslike design. The game focused on shooting enemies and using melee options as a backup, to try and free the Earth and other dimensions from an invasion by a cosmic force. The game made use of procedural generation by stitching different environmental areas together to create a level. The flow of the game had the player moving through several main areas before coming to a dungeon, which was also procedurally generated. At the end of it, players had to fight one of several randomly chosen bosses, with each boss having a reward in the form of a new weapon to use, or weapon mod that could be attached to a player's gun. Due to the focus on ranged combat, the game would regularly generate enemy groups to attack the player that would drop different ammo types. The unique take on soulslike design earned the game praise from fans and critics, and the developers released a sequel in 2023 (Figure 5.17).

5. How From Software Defined Soulslikes

Code Vein developed by Bandai Namco was a soulslike that focused more on character customization. The player's character could absorb different blood codes from enemies that would confer different benefits and special attacks. The game made it very easy for the player to switch between different builds and play-styles simply adjusting what blood codes they were using with advanced customization by picking the exact codes around a specific strategy or playstyle.

In a surprising move, the Star Wars **IP** would get their own take with *Star Wars Jedi: Fallen Order* in 2019 developed by Respawn Entertainment. Taking the soulslike formula and translating it into being a Jedi in an original story set in the Star Wars universe. The game did well enough to get a sequel with the subtitle: Survivor in 2023.

By 2020, the genre conventions of soulslikes were set, and with the successes of the *Dark Souls* trilogy, fewer studios were making them to avoid competing with From Software who continued to have hit after hit. This year, there were only two major examples released that each did their own thing with the design. *Mortal Shell* by Cold Symmetry did something that no other soulslike to date attempted – create a condensed and short soulslike. Players controlled a strange being who would inhabit shells of former warriors to explore the world and try to defeat the bosses and creatures that lived there. Using the ability to "harden," the character could become a stone statue to completely mitigate damage and set up to counterattack the opposing enemy. Unlike other souls-likes, there was a set limit of customization options built around the different shells and a few weapon types. With only a few major areas to explore and the hub, the game was by far the shortest soulslike to be released. Then there was the game *Hellpoint* released by Cradle Games that took place in the far future on a space station where everyone was killed. With a greater focus on platforming alongside combat, the game did suffer from balancing issues and the platforming being a bit hard to do. While finishing writing this book, the number of 3D soulslikes released have shrunk, with the last one I played being *Lies of P* released in 2023 by Neowiz.

As I said at the start of this section, part of the marketing of soulslikes was describing every difficult game as one. Games like *Dark Devotion* released in 2019 by Hibernian Workshop was a challenging 2D game to play that also borrowed elements of soulslike design. A popular subgenre that also saw some renewed interest with the "Dark Souls" comparison was the "boss rush." This is a kind of game where there are no minor enemies for the player to fight, every battle is with a unique boss and there is often nothing else to the game beyond it. Another reason why this became popular was the trend of games using the words "Dark" or "Souls" as part of their titles to invoke the sense that these games were soulslikes or just very difficult (Figure 5.18). *Titan Souls* released in 2015 by Acid Nerve tasked players to hunt down giant creatures with the twist being that everything died to a single hit. The player's character controlled a magic arrow that they would need to get a shot at the monster's weak point to kill it before they were killed. *Eldest Souls* released in 2021 by Fallen Flag Studio took this concept

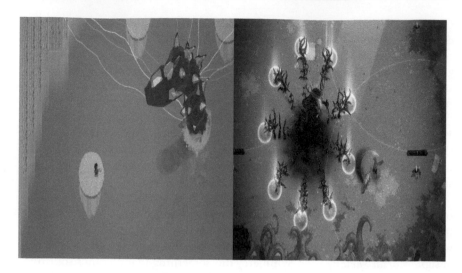

Figure 5.18

You would not believe the number of games released in the 2010s that had either "Dark" or "Souls" somewhere in its title. With *Titan Souls* and *Eldest Souls* (released in 2015 by Acid Nerve, and in 2021 by Fallen Flag Studio, respectively), they embodied difficult, boss rush design, but also struggled to reach a wider market due to their difficulty.

further and gave the player customization options and different ways of fighting the game's variety of incredibly challenging bosses.

There are plenty of other games large and small that were either soulslike in passing or tried to use the marketing of it, but this section is starting to feel long enough already. Before I move on, there are two important aspects of the market that need to be discussed. As I said earlier, as the decade went on, fewer souslikes were being released. This is what happened with the platformer genre in the AAA space, and how studios became afraid to compete against Nintendo with the *Mario* franchise. To this day, From Software did not have one poorly reviewed soulslike released, and as I mentioned, each new entry from them became the defining standard of the genre that everyone else was being judged by. Games like *Salt and Sanctuary* and *Remnant: From the Ashes* succeeded by being legitimately different experiences that From Software was not aiming for with their games. The *Nioh* series is considered #2 by fans of the genre due to the increased focus on combat. However, none of those series come close to the sales and reception that each *Dark Souls* game received during the 2010s. When I discuss *Elden Ring* at the end of this book, I will examine how From Software has raised the bar even higher from other studios.

The other points I want to mention, and something that will be discussed more in the next chapter and Chapter 8, are the core elements that must be in a game for it to be considered a soulslike, and more specifically, a ***good one***. Every

5. How From Software Defined Soulslikes

soulslike must have proper level design, a great combat system, and character abstracted progression to go with the combat. Many of the soulslikes that came out during the decade never managed to hit all three points the same way that From Software did. Some focused on level design, but the combat was lacking; others did a great job with their combat, but the level design wasn't as strong or the RPG progression didn't work right. This is not an easy subgenre to make a game in and requires an almost cross-discipline knowledge of design to do right.

5.5 Why Did the Soulslike Genre Blow Up?

For the last part of this chapter, it's time to sum up how From Software essentially created a new market of games and became the posterchild for it. The video-game market is a constantly evolving and hard-to-predict entity. Sometimes, the difference between a game becoming a multimillion-dollar success and barely scratching 1,000 copies sold can come down to timing. In 2009, with the original *Demon's Souls*, there were several trends happening in the game industry that helped the game stand out. As I talked about at the start of this chapter, the 2000s, specifically the tail end of it, was marked by two AAA trends:

1. Major studios were focusing on multiplayer experiences designed around long-term engagement and monetization.
2. Developers were moving away from challenging titles to focus on those with broader appeals.

People who only grew up playing games in the 2010s will usually point out that soulslikes are very difficult games, but anyone who played older titles in the '90s into the 2000s should remember that titles were designed to be far more difficult (Figure 5.19). This is why I'm going to be dedicating an entire chapter to the discussion of difficulty design, and why designing a challenging game is different than designing a hard game. Many older titles had poor user interface and user experience (**UI/UX**); either because of limitations of hardware or the fact that design standards weren't implemented yet.

Hardware is another point about From Software's success. A game like *Demon Souls* could have never been made in that way in the 90s. Early gamepads as I talked about were not designed around full 3D movement, and the first generation of 3D consoles did not have the power to keep a steady framerate when a lot was being rendered on screen at once. Even on the PlayStation 3, *Demon's Souls* still had framerate issues and so did *Dark Souls*. It would take indie developers with the increased power and functionality of free game engines, several more years before they could attempt to make 3D soulslikes.

The push by developers to focus on multiplayer experiences over single player is another factor. For you reading this now, especially after the 2010s, it's hard to remember a time when single-player games were not popular. But during the 2000s and the first half of the 2010s, studios were trying to capitalize on the live

Figure 5.19

There are a lot of games from the 90s that were known for being quite difficult at their time. Some were hard because they challenged the player; others due to balancing and pacing issues, and some just did a horrible job of explaining what was going on. The system of running out of lives was huge for arcades and early video games to punish players for failing and forcing them to restart the entire game.

service trend that first began with MMORPGs, to the booming mobile scene, and of course the success of games like *Call of Duty* (many different release dates and published by Activision) and *League of Legends* (released in 2009 by Riot Games). In *Game Design Deep Dive: Horror* I touched on how this trend impacted the horror space and led it to all but disappearing in the 2010s from major studios, while indies went in their own direction to create a new horror game scene.

The market can be fickle at times and *Demon's Souls* owes its success not only to having great gameplay but coming out to prove that consumers still wanted challenging games; that there was still indeed a market for predominantly single-player experiences (Figure 5.20). There were many talks and presentations given during the 2010s on how live service design, and especially mobile design, was going to be the next gold rush that would change videogames forever. What we saw play out was anything but – the major names in mobile and live service continued to make lots of money, but the market became a case of oases in a desert. So many AAA and indie titles that tried to chase this trend have gone under, and instead, we have seen from about 2015 on a return to form for single player–driven experiences. There are other successful single-player games that stood out in the 2010s, but we could certainly argue that From Software's souls-likes did make a huge case for having games that weren't built around live service design. If you are interested more in the history of mobile design and monetization, please read *Game Design Deep Dive: F2P*.

Figure 5.20

Many developers and studios thought the future of the game industry was in online and live service games. Instead, we saw more movement from studios to make unique single-player experiences with far too many to list here. I wouldn't say that *Dark Souls* and soulslikes are the sole reason for this, but the success did blindside a lot of studios who were focusing on live service games.

6

Intro to Soulslikes

6.1 What Is a Soulslike?

Thankfully, defining what is a soulslike is going to be far easier than trying to define what an RPG is from my previous Deep Dive. Being considered a sub-genre like metroidvanias means that there are specific design qualifiers that must be present for a game to be called a soulslike (Figure 6.1). In the last chapter, I brought up the three pillars of design and I want to explain them a little more in depth before we talk about the implementation and philosophy in Chapter 8.

Let's start with combat. What separates a soulslike from what would be considered a full-action title is that the player's character is supposed to be kept at the same level as all the enemies in the game. In titles that are built around action, like the *Devil May Cries, Dooms, God of Wars*, and so on, the main character is considered the most powerful force in the game. They are supposed to be faster, more reactive, and stronger than anything else.

For a soulslike to work, every character must be on the same level in terms of combat pacing. The combat speed in a soulslike is noticeably slower than in action titles; with *Nioh's* and *Wo Long's* design being the closest to a full-on action title.

DOI: 10.1201/9781003450078-6

Figure 6.1

Many people look at *Sekiro*'s design and structure and immediately label it a souls-like. However, of From Software's games released in the 2010s, its design skews more toward an action game as it lacks the variety of progression seen in soulslike examples.

Instead of it feeling awkward or slow-paced, what makes the soulslike combat work is this emphasis on the impact of hitting an enemy.

Every weapon has its own swing and timing to be used effectively, and just mashing the attack button in these games is not going to work out. Part of this is how many soulslikes have a way of limiting how aggressive a character can be. On the player's side, this is often achieved by having a resource that dictates how often they can attack via a "stamina" system. Every offensive and defensive action will cost stamina, if the character runs out of it, they are unable to perform these actions, and why it can be death when they do. Depending on the game's design and the focus of the combat, will determine the extent in which stamina drains and recovers, if the system is featured at all.

The other way to institute a soulslike-styled pacing is with the animations themselves. I already mentioned the concept of input buffering earlier in the book and how it once again punishes button mashing. There needs to be a sense of "weight" or "heft" to combat. Swinging a knife should be far faster than swinging a heavy longsword. This is how the different games have pseudo classes to them, as each weapon behaves differently in a fight. Part of the difficulty of designing a combat system like this is that there must be an inherent balance between using lighter and faster weapons vs. weapons that are heavier and take longer to swing. This is something that will come up again in Chapter 8.

From an enemy design point of view, they must be built to provide different degrees of challenge – even the "weakest" enemy in a soulslike can still take out someone who is inexperienced at the game (Figure 6.2). The threat level of an

Figure 6.2

The first enemies in any soulslike are there to teach the player that this is not a traditional action game, but in the grand scheme of the playthrough, are just quick roadblocks to someone who knows what they are doing.

enemy is dependent on their response to the player's attacks. If the enemy has no response, then the player can keep attacking them until either it dies, or the player's character runs out of stamina. This is once again referred to as a stun lock. Some games will have it set up that if a character is hit X number of times in a row, they will automatically dodge away or perform a counterattack to prevent the player from continuing to hit them. For stronger enemies and bosses, they will not get stunned by normal attacks, only heavier attacks or special skills may work. For the player, they must focus on dodging or blocking attacks to get a quick swing off, before returning to defending. There are more advanced elements of enemy design that I will come back to later in the book.

The second point is about character progression and soulslikes are set up to accommodate different ways of building a character. This can be allocating every stat point earned to build a fully customized character. A simpler example would be just providing them with different weapons and gear that focus on specific ways of playing. As an extension of the previous point about combat, many souslikes feature specific styles of play – melee, ranged, spellcaster, etc. These can be further exemplified by having the ability to unlock passive bonuses or "perks" that can enhance a character further. The important detail of this category is that there must be different, **and viable**, ways of approaching the game. Returning to *Sekiro*, while the game does meet the standard for combat and level design (that will come up next), it's not built to be played in different way, if the player doesn't learn the parry system, there is nothing else that will let them win the game. You can argue that the different items available do provide alternative ways of

6. Intro to Soulslikes

Figure 6.3

The first stage of *Demon's Souls* is a great example to study in terms of the flow and pacing of a soulslike level. Later games would evolve the size and complexity of the level design, notably by including more side routes and alternate paths around. This became important due to the world design becoming interconnected as things went on.

fighting, but every aspect of *Sekiro*'s design is built off the parrying – the player either learns it, or they're not going to be able to finish the game.

For the final point, and one that hasn't been discussed yet, is the specific kind of level design present in these games. Besides the overall structure of the world that will be discussed later in this book, soulslikes feature a specific kind of level design focused on shortcuts and denser areas. When we examine traditional level design in reflex-driven games, a level is made up of a specific beginning, middle, and end point – as someone moves through each part of the level, the previous part no longer matters. This is where people like to poke fun at modern-day first-person shooters and describe their levels as a straight corridor. Many action games treat their levels as just a series of arenas – the player enters a new room, the doors lock, and the player can't move on until they have defeated every enemy in there. In a soulslike, levels are designed around various sections that connect to one another. Because the player will always return to a bonfire as their respawn point, progress in the stage must be preserved another way via shortcuts. Anytime the player opens a shortcut, it remains permanently open. Some shortcuts are there to skip a tough section in a stage, or literally bypass the entire stage once the player reaches the end.

A great example of this comes from *Demon's Souls* first stage, or 1-1. The stage is structured around a massive castle with two towers on either side of the main gate (Figure 6.3). Both towers have locked doors at the start. The player must first go left of the door, fight their way through courtyards and up the battlements, to reach the left tower and open its door. From that point, the entire first quarter of the stage is now skippable. The next path is from the left tower to cross through more open areas, dodge a dragon, and fight their way to the right-side tower that has the lever that opens the main gate. Once the main gate is open, the player now has instant access to the boss of the stage directly from the beginning. This kind of structure is a mainstay in every From Software soulslike and is an important aspect of the risk/reward of their design. If someone wants to run back to the bonfire and spend their souls, they can do that at the consequence of respawning every enemy they fought. But if they push forward and get that next shortcut open, then they have officially made progress that will not be lost. Level design in this respect wraps around itself as opposed to the player just moving further and further away from the start point.

When the design evolved with *Dark Souls* and up to *Elden Ring*, this kind of design was still there, but now everything shares the same world. With this redesign, there are two kinds of areas in these games – areas that are meant to be run through to get to the next major point, and then the areas that are actual stages with shortcuts and a boss to fight. In Section 8.1, I'll discuss more about environmental and level design.

In the last chapter, I mentioned that one of the reasons why no one else has come close to From Software's success in the soulslike genre has been how well they have managed these three points. Where a lot of developers struggled with their soulslikes is with the combat system. Anytime we talk about reflex-driven gameplay, there is a very specific feel that you are trying to evoke out of your game regardless of your genre and gameplay loop. You want the player to feel like they are completely in control of their character, and that they don't do anything that the player didn't command them to. This is part of why the pacing that From Software defined has worked so well. Because every player is tied to the same exact pacing of their character, it means that while having good reflexes is an important aspect of playing these games, it is not as fast-paced as a traditional action game.

Another area where developers have failed trying to emulate From Software is with difficulty and how it goes together with the combat system. I'll discuss more about difficulty in the next chapter, but it does have a specific relation to how the gameplay and combat play out. The player needs to feel that they are given the tools and combat options needed to fight any enemy in the game. There is a huge difference between the player knowing that they aren't good enough yet to win an encounter versus the feeling like the game is actively against them at the gameplay layer. If you have a game that is built on dodging attacks, and the enemies are designed to track the player so well with their attack patterns that dodging is all but useless, then the player is going to feel like the game is broken and won't play it.

With difficulty, one of the worst mistakes that you can make as a designer trying to make a soulslike is approaching your design to make it as difficult as possible. There are two reasons why From Software can get away with some pain points and difficulty spikes that other developers cannot. First, their games are

Figure 6.4

From Software as a studio is one of the few who can get away with very challenging boss fights and situations for the most part. In *Armored Core 6: Fires of Rubicon*, it is a game that demands a lot out of the player, and why the boss here caused so many people problems. However, understanding when something is too much or too little of a challenge is a major aspect of difficulty balance that I'll talk about in the next chapter.

balanced in a way that a player who is good enough at the game and understands the gameplay can get past any challenge (Figure 6.4). Too often, developers will make enemy and boss encounters that clash with the pacing set by the player's character. These fights are still beatable, but it's not a case of the player becoming better at the game but exploiting a specific way of playing to win. Here is a good example of this – the act of parrying. I have personally played many action games and soulslikes where parrying is the be-all, end-all skill to beat the game. Even if it is supposed to be the riskiest option, due to the design of the enemies and the rest of the player's options, it is far and away the best way of playing the game and can trivialize any encounter. You may think that having an option so good is fine, but if everything else doesn't work or is just simply not good enough to be used in the game, players will become frustrated and bored with your design.

The other reason why From Software can get away with some issues is something that no other developer reading this will be able to match – the clout of the studio. Gamedev is too big of a field to cover in these books, but I want to touch on an important lesson for designers. Whichever studio is the first to market a new genre or type of gameplay becomes the standard bearer of it. They are allowed to make mistakes or have issues with their games because they were the first. If/when they become successful with their designs, they can reach a level of prestige with their games that no one else in the genre can get to, and this point will come back when I talk about *Elden Ring*.

With level design and RPG progression, they are also important, but if your game can't get the combat right, then neither of those points is going to redeem your game. When you are building your levels, there must be a flow and structure to them. Making every room literally look alike doesn't work, neither does every room looking like it comes from a different game. You need to set up proper checkpoints and provide the player with ways of making progress.

Building out your character is a tough point, and a lot of the balancing and design of RPG gameplay in general can be found in my Deep Dive. For soulslikes specifically, you want to give the player enough options that are viable for playing the game. If you're going to do something that is unique for character development; such as *The Surge*'s different modules or *Code Vein*'s blood codes, then that needs to be clearly articulated to the player.

While I will be breaking down more aspects of action design in relation to soulslikes, there is a lot more to the kind of design that will be saved for a Deep Dive specifically on the genre.

6.2 Defining Action and Abstracted Progression

Soulslikes are both about action and abstracted design, and why they fit within a specific style of a subgenre (Figure 6.5). And because of that, I won't be going

Figure 6.5

The merging of reflex-driven and abstracted design became popular in the 2010s, as more action games added in RPG progression, like *Borderlands 3* (released in 2019 by Gearbox Software), and more RPGs started to become more action-oriented, such as *Final Fantasy 15* (released in 2016 by Square Enix). This led to new designs, and a new audience for these kinds of games.

into extreme detail about both forms of design. For a more encompassing discussion about abstracted design, please read *Game Design Deep Dive: Role Playing Games.*

Action, or as I define it as reflex-driven gameplay, focuses on the player's own skills and reactions as the primary form of progression. This requires good reflexes and depending on the difficulty of the game, having a good APM or actions per minute. Reflex-driven gameplay forms the basis of all action genres. On the extreme end of this design, these are the fans who always want to be the one who decides whether they win or lose. For soulslikes, it has given them a negative impression of fans who attack critics of the genre with the now famous phrase "git gud." Reflex-driven gameplay does have a limit in terms of its audience. The more difficult a game is to play, the fewer people will be able to play it at that level. Many of the best action games released in the 2000s also came with incredibly high difficulty curves that stopped people from beating them.

Abstracted design is when the rules and attributes within the game dictate success or failure. In a turn-based game, how fast someone reacts has no bearing on whether their character is going to score a hit. Instead of the player getting better to define progression, it is about growing the strength of the character that will determine success. This can be achieved through different systems such as leveling up, getting new equipment, attaching perks to a character, and more. The abstracted design has no upper limit to it or specific rules for what must be included. The limitation of abstracted progression is that there will always come a point where the value of the numbers, or abstraction, loses meaning to the player. Going from doing 5 points of damage to 50 is a huge jump; going from 3,343,232 to 4,121,756 doesn't have the same impact.

What From Software did with *Demon's Souls* was to create a new design trend of merging both designs as closely as they could. The reflex-driven gameplay rewards people who are good at reacting to challenges and gives an intrinsic reward to the player that they themselves are improving at the game. Using abstracted progression provides more depth to character customization and gives someone another way of making progress in the game (Figure 6.6). If someone gets stuck in an action game and can't improve their skills, then the game is over for them. But with abstracted progression, they can enhance their character to compensate and provide another way to get around a difficult challenge.

The beauty of this double approach is that both forms of progression are legitimate ways of playing a soulslike. If someone is good enough at the game that they can just use the starting weapons and beat every single fight, then that works for them. Conversely, if someone needs to upgrade all their gear, keep raising their attributes up, and then demolishes enemies with that power, then that's also a fair way to play. The middle ground that soulslikes occupy between the two forms of progression is that the player is in complete control of their character and the reactions that occur during combat. Where the abstraction matters is what happens when the player hits an enemy or is struck by one, that's when the RPG systems come into play to dictate what happens next. In a game that has a greater

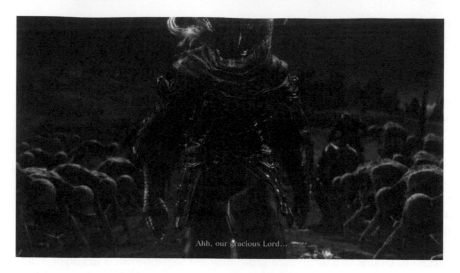

Ahh, our gracious Lord...

Figure 6.6

The thrill of playing a soulslike is about conquering the challenges of the game in a way that best suits the player. While From Software has eased up a little bit on the skill needed to beat their games compared to action and first-person shooters, it is still an accomplishment to see them all the way through to the end.

focus on the RPG systems, the abstracted elements would matter at the moment the player tries to do something, such as swinging a sword, and the game calculating if that attack would connect.

This trend of combining abstracted progression with other genres and designs blew up in the 2010s with the rise of mobile and live service games. While reflex-driven gameplay does have that upper limit of what the player can do, abstracted progression can be extended indefinitely, and has been a part of many of the most successful mobile and live service games. The action and shooter genres have also seen more aspects of abstract progression added to them. *God of War 2018* and *God of War: Ragnarok* (both released in 2022 by Santa Monica Studio), introduced abstract progression with finding equipment of different levels to boost the overall strength of Kratos. Both *Doom 2016* and *Doom Eternal* (released in 2020 by id Software) introduced ways of permanently enhancing the main character outside of the player getting better at the game.

Today, it is considered odd not to have abstracted progression in an action title, and even the modern *Final Fantasies* have focused on being action games with RPG progression. The challenge of these two forms of progression is that for a soulslike to work, both must be given ample room to work. Many soulslikes get progressively easier over the course of playing thanks to the player getting better at the reflex-side of things, and then upgrading their build to go even further. Conversely, it means that the opening of these games is often the hardest and where they lose a lot of their player base. As the designer, you need to be careful

6. Intro to Soulslikes

about how much you lean into requiring reflex or abstracted progression with your gameplay. If you introduce enemies that require high-level reflexes to win, and there aren't abstracted options available, that can easily end your experience for RPG fans. Conversely, pushing enemy attributes so far that the game becomes tiresome to play unless someone grinds can also ruin the experience. Getting this balance of difficulty and the skill curve right is not easy to do and is again why Chapter 7 of this book is going to be dedicated to difficulty design.

6.3 Weapon Design

I've spoken a lot about combat throughout this book, but it's also important to understand how the weapons you design feed into both the customization and the balance of your combat system. There is no rule for the number of weapons you must include in your game. Some titles may focus on a generic and wide pool of weapons that have basic differences to their attributes. Other games may have a smaller pool, but each weapon is legitimately a different way of playing through the game (Figure 6.7).

Here are some of the basic attributes that you should consider when building and balancing the weapons in your game:

Figure 6.7

The design of your weapons will play a huge role in defining how combat and your gameplay will turn out. In this game: *Asterigos: Curse of the stars* (released in 2022 by Acme GameStudio), each weapon is entirely a one-off – with different special abilities and playstyles. In this approach, the weapons are akin to choosing a class in an RPG. The goal is to design each weapon so that someone who plays a game will have "their favorite" that they can take through the entire game.

- Weapon Type: The type of weapon and how it interacts with other elements.
- Damage Type: The type of damage of the weapon.
- Damage Value: The amount of damage it will do.
- Requirements to use the weapon: What attribute thresholds are needed to use it?
- Attack Speed: How fast the weapon is, or how quickly the attack animation plays out.
- One or Two Handed: Whether this weapon can be wielded with one or both hands.
- Hit Stun: Does this weapon stun or stagger the enemy, and by how much?

The weapon type is what classification the weapon belong to, and the importance of this is going to be dependent on your design. In soulslikes that have special buffs or equipment that boosts specific weapon types, this is how the player will know which weapons will benefit from what. In other games, the weapon type can be more diverse, such as weapons that belong to unique types that each have their own rules or behavior for using them. A simple example would be ranged weapons that require a specific ammo to be used. While not a soulslike, the *Monster Hunter* franchise by Capcom breaks down each one of its weapons by different types, and then by variations of that type. Two greatswords will function the same way but could have vastly different attributes, but a greatsword and a bow gun are fundamentally different.

Damage type is something that is always important and another way that weapons can differ from one another. In games where enemies are designed to be stronger or weaker to specific damage types, this is important to convey to the player. One thing to note, just because weapons can belong to the same type of weapon, does not mean that they all must share the same damage type. Many of the unique weapons featured in each From Software soulslike will have a completely different damage type compared to their contemporaries in the same grouping, like a club that could cause pierce damage instead of blunt. The more damage types you have in your game, the more ways you're going to need to design enemies to be affected by them.

The amount of damage is the easiest one to understand on this list, but how you determine this will be dependent on the other attributes. Everything from the damage type, to the swing of the weapon and its weight will factor in. Remember this point – the base damage of a weapon is not always the most important aspect of it. Having a superfast attack could be more useful against faster enemies compared to a weapon that does more damage but is slower. In games where weapons can have additional effects, it may be worth it to use a weaker weapon if it does more than cause damage.

The requirements to use a weapon is another aspect that greatly varies between games. A simple example is with having a perk tree system with weapon usage tied to different passives. Returning to *Salt and Sanctuary*, every weapon and

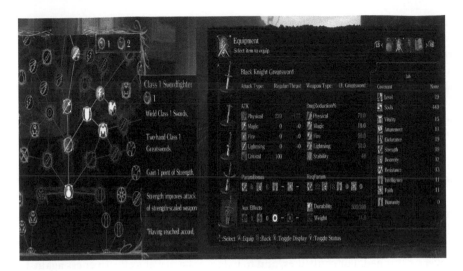

Figure 6.8

How you define gear progression is another aspect of abstracted design. In *Salt and Sanctuary* on the left, the player, by design, is supposed to find a weapon type they like and continue to go up the respective tier list to gain more power. In *Dark Souls* on the right, the character's attributes are what limits what weapons the player can use effectively, but once they find one they like and have the prerequisite attribute points, then they can stay with it and continue to upgrade it.

piece of gear had a tier rating and an equipment type. For a character to use a tier 2 knife, they would need to unlock the corresponding perk on their skill tree. It did not matter as to what any other attribute was on a character, without the right perk that weapon would be borderline useless. The other way of handling requirements is tying it to character attributes, and this can also affect scaling that I mentioned in Section 4.2 (Figure 6.8). By building requirements this way it hammers home the point that characters must be built around specific builds. If a giant sword requires 45 strength, and a magic staff needs 35 intelligence, the chance of a character being built to use both is very low.

Attack speed directly impacts the damage per second, or DPS, of a weapon. Faster weapons mean that the player can perform more attacks compared to a slower weapon and is able to react faster to the enemy. To balance this, designers will set fast weapons to have an overall lower damage value, under the assumption that the weapon will be swung more to compensate. The attack speed really matters when it comes to stunning an enemy that I'll talk more about further down. The more times the player can hit in a row, the easier it will be to inflict debuffs or other aliments on an enemy.

One or two-handed weapons are another abstracted element that also factors into different builds. A one-handed weapon means that the weapon can be used alongside something else in the character's other hand. That could be anything from a lantern to provide light, a shield to block damage, and so on. Two-handed weapons are meant to be larger, do far more damage, but also come with greater restrictions on using them. Swinging a knife should be a lot easier than lifting a giant club. One of the details that From Software did with their weapons in this regard was design "great" or "colossal" weapons – weapons designed to be so heavy and have stat requirements so high, that no starting character could use them one-handed. It was possible to build a character so focused on that one attribute that they could use them one-handed, but there was another way. Whatever the stat requirement a weapon has would be cut in half if the player held it with two hands. For example – a giant's club had a 40-strength requirement, if the player used it with both hands, that requirement became 20 strength.

Hit stun greatly varies between soulslikes and traditional action games. In most action titles, the ability to stun the enemy with your attacks is dependent on the enemy and not the weapon. This is when every minor enemy can always be stunned if you get a hit in, and every elite or boss-class enemy will never be stunned. For soulslikes, and to balance the player's effectiveness against the enemy, there are different rules and methods for how this can work. On the basic side, weapons can simply be programmed to stun or stagger someone when they are struck by it. Typically, faster and weaker weapons wouldn't be able to stun, while landing a blow with a heavy weapon will make the enemy stop for a second. Another way is that weapons have a certain number of "stagger" that is applied when they hit an enemy. The enemy has their own stagger meter, which some games make invisible to the player. When the enemy's stagger meter maxes out, they become stunned by the attack. Not only can a weapon have a stagger rating, but so can the type of attack used. In games where there is a light and heavy attack for each weapon, the heavy attack will have more stagger dealt to the enemy. In *Elden Ring*, one of the new attack types introduced was a jump attack that did heavy stagger damage to an enemy. Being able to stop the enemy from attacking needs to be decided while you are building your combat system, because this will determine what attacks and strategies will be effective in your game. If the player cannot stop the enemy from doing their attack, then slower attacks, or ones that can't be canceled out of, will be borderline useless. If certain enemies can't be staggered at all, then combat will revolve around stick and move strategies (Figure 6.9).

There are other attributes you can have on weapons depending on how advanced your combat system is. One that I didn't mention that is often polarizing among fans is "durability," or how long a weapon can be used before it loses its effectiveness. Some of From Software's games have used durability, but later entries have removed this as many felt it was just an unnecessary constraint on a game that is hard enough already.

If your game is going to measure the overall weight a character is carrying on them, then you will also need to assign a weight to every weapon as well. Once again, the heavier the weapon should mean that the weapon does more damage.

Figure 6.9

Elden Ring featured a lot of bosses where it was very hard to trade damage with them. Starscourge Radahn is as fast as he is huge, and standing still is a good way to get hit in the face. This is a fight where you're going to have to battle for every hit you get in if you're fighting him at close range.

Another attribute that greatly depends on the design is how aliments or debuffs will work. A common element in RPGs is to have skills or weapons that can have additional effects on the enemy; such as poisoning them, burning, freezing, shocking, and many others. In a turn-based game, attributes can either be applied as a percentage chance on each hit, or just trigger on a single use. For soulslikes, they will often tie aliments to filling up an inflict bar. Every time the weapon hits, the bar fills up a little more; when it's completely full, the aliment is applied. If someone is resistant to that aliment, it may take more hits to fill it up, or they could just be completely immune to it. Once again, this information may be hidden from the player during combat.

Whether or not you want to create unique weapons or a large pool of generic weapons is entirely up to you and the design you are aiming for. The more weapons in your game will mean that there are far more options for players to create a character around, and the more balancing that will need to be done. Most of From Software's games feature a mix of both – generic weapons that can be bought and found, and unique weapons tied to specific rewards and challenges. In this respect, the unique weapons will not only look differently compared to similar ones but could have vastly different properties to them. A popular example is giving a weapon a completely different damage type or property not associated to it – like a dagger that can cause poison or bleed instead of just normal slash damage (Figure 6.10). Going fully unique, such as in *Bloodborne*'s case, means that

Figure 6.10

Unique weapons that break the normal rules of combat can be fun things to add to your game and provide another way of creating a build. With Reduvia, being able to create long-range attacks with a traditionally short-range weapon is a great touch.

you can get far more creative with each individual weapon, but that also means that there are far fewer ways of building a character.

Another point about weapon design that you will need to consider is whether there is progression tied to different weapons of the same type. As discussed in *Game Design Deep Dive: Role Playing Games*, many RPGs will create progression via different versions of the same weapon, such as going from an iron sword to a sliver sword. The other way of progression with weapons is allowing the player to upgrade their level via a blacksmith or some other secondary system. This is an important decision for soulslikes due to how reflex-intensive they are. If someone gets used to swinging an axe, and then they are forced to use a sword due to not being able to keep powering up the axe, it can throw off their entire sense of rhythm. In the *Dark Souls* series, while there are different versions of each weapon type, they are considered side-grades rather than just one replacing the other. Such as having swords that handle differently, have different attribute scaling, and how they are swung. This way, if the player finds a weapon they like, they can keep using it and not feel like they are being punished for not switching. A fundamental difference between a soulslike and a standard ARPG (action role-playing game) is that ARPG design is about the player frequently finding new gear that they will replace what they are using to become stronger. Due to the reflex-driven nature of soulslikes, most players will look for a specific weapon or type of weapon that they like to use, and then stick with that. This is also helped by the fact that soulslikes will not typically procedurally generate gear, except for *Nioh*'s design.

For the final point, being able to create inventive or unique weapons can be a way for your game to stand out. With so many soulslikes that have focused on traditional fantasy/medieval weapons, doing something differently, like futuristic with *The Surge*, is a way to distinguish your game from other examples. However, if your combat system doesn't work right, then all the interesting weapon designs will be for naught, and why I'll be focusing on the pacing of a soulslike in Section 8.3.

7

A Study of Difficulty

7.1 Difficulty vs. Depth

It's time for the customary Deep Dive super long chapter where I spend a lot of time on a single topic (Figure 7.1). In each book I've written, I've spoken distantly about the difficulty and left that up to you reading to figure out how hard you want to make your game, but talking about soulslikes is different. The genre and From Software became famous due to coming out during a period when games were moving away from challenging gameplay as I talked about in Chapter 5.

Difficulty is an inherent part of soulslike design and of game design. It's something that many people, both within and outside of game development, tend to not fully understand the implications and philosophy of. While this chapter is going to be about soulslikes, the discussion itself can be applied to any game design and any genre in terms of difficulty.

The first lesson I want to touch on is how difficulty and depth are not one and the same. One of the mistakes a lot of designers have made trying to copy soulslike design, and even roguelike design, has been thinking that difficulty is a measure of quality. As I mentioned earlier in this book with the phrase "git gud," there are fans of any hard game who believe that because the game was

DOI: 10.1201/9781003450078-7

Figure 7.1

Difficulty and challenge are essential aspects to understand if you want to build any reflex-driven game. There is an infinite number of ways of making a game hard or challenging but doing it in a way that breaks your gameplay will leave you with a lot of frustrated consumers. The Marauder from *Doom Eternal* was one of the most polarizing additions to the game due to how different it was to fight, and people are still arguing whether it was a well-designed enemy.

hard, it was also good. This is the same vocal minority who will attack critics or consumers who want to see things made easier or accessibility and approachability features added to a game. I will be talking more about approachability in Section 8.3.

A fundamental lesson I've spoken and written at length about is that difficulty – either very easy or very hard – is quite easy to accomplish. If I'm designing an action game and I give the player five points of health and make every enemy do 100 points of damage, then that would be a very hard experience, right? Just as I could add in an "easy mode" where the player has 5,000 points of health and every enemy would only do 1 point of damage. For both these examples, it is possible that there is a small contingent of fans who would like modes like that, but the general consumer is not going to appreciate a game that is too punishing or one that there is no need for any interaction with the mechanics.

On that last point, there was a period where designers were pushing the idea of a "story mode" as a way of playing a game without needing to be challenged by it or interact with it. I am also not a fan of this, because at the end of the day, if the only way for someone to play your game is to turn off all your game systems to enjoy it, then your game systems are inherently flawed or not balanced right. There is an exception to this that I'll come back to in Section 7.3 with assist and sandbox mode options. The reason why this is okay is if a game has different

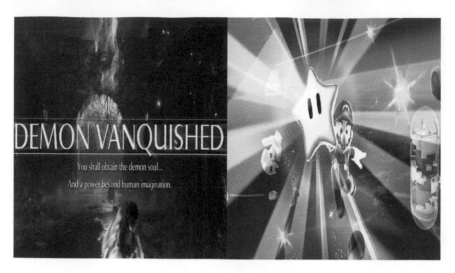

Figure 7.2

A part of soulslike design or any game built on the reflex-driven challenge is the intrinsic reward of the player knowing they are getting better at the game and this affects how they play. This is very hard to design into a game, and there must be ways of showing the player's skills are growing. In *Demon's Souls* and soulslikes, it's how the games become easier once the player knows what to do. In a platformer like *Super Mario Galaxy* (released in 2007 by Nintendo), as someone becomes better at the game, they can move through the levels differently.

ways of playing it that can appeal to different audiences. For our discussion on soulslike and reflex-driven design, there are elements that are intrinsic to the gameplay loop that if you don't do right or remove, then you are failing the genre qualifiers. Conversely, if playing the game on the highest level of difficulty feels like the gameplay is broken due to imbalances, then people are also going to feel that the game wasn't properly designed. Someone can stop playing a game because they find it too difficult, or they can stop playing if they find that the game is not engaging them. Many designers will tout sales numbers or critical accolades to counter this, but the achievement rates tell another story. Most video games will lose the bulk of their consumer base within the first hour; with the majority occurring within 30 minutes. The reason is that this is the time frame where all the pain points and issues in your game will become known to the consumer, and if they're not enjoying the game now, then there's no reason to keep sticking with it.

The real challenge as a game designer is to create a balanced experience – one where the player is given all the tools and elements needed to succeed and they feel that they are improving at the game (Figure 7.2). To move the player through a game and learn its mechanics, there must be ***depth, not difficulty,*** to the gameplay. What made the original *Demon's Souls* work was that there was challenge and depth to the combat system. It wasn't hard to learn how to swing a sword or block an attack, but the player had to learn the intricacies of each weapon if they wanted to succeed. This is why the pacing and UI/UX for a soulslike are important to get correct, if someone feels like the gameplay itself is getting in the way of being able to play it, they're not going to keep struggling with it.

Too many designers and gamers think that difficulty makes for a good experience, but if there is no depth to the mechanics, then all you have is something that is difficult for difficulty's sake. There have been several surprise hits from indie developers over the 2010s in the form of "rage games." Games that were meant to purposely be frustrating and punishing to play. The most famous being *Getting Over It With Bennett Foddy* released in 2017. The game caught on thanks to becoming a "badge of honor" to get through, and how so many streamers and Youtubers covered it and made "rage videos." That "badge of honor" is something to take note of, as it is often the rationale to praise difficulty in games. There will always be people who like to play hard games over easy ones, myself included there. However, I do not like to play games where it's just plain difficult as opposed to there being an interesting challenge.

The difference between depth and difficulty is that depth means there is more going on with the game – that the player needs to learn the mechanics and rules if they want to succeed, and that there are more ways to win if you understand what's happening. Just adjusting stats to make something easier or harder does not change the inherent nature of the design. Returning to RPG progression, at some point in every abstracted progression system, numbers start to lose their meaning. Part of understanding the difference between difficulty and depth means comprehending why something is difficult in the first place. Is it hard because the game is challenging the player? Or it is hard because the UI/UX isn't working, the gameplay is not being explained well, or is frustrating to perform?

To that point, it's why I'm very leery of designers who think that difficulty settings are the answer to any game where people say that something is difficult. If a game is difficult because the controls don't feel right, or the character is awkward to fight with, having an easy, medium, and hard mode is not going to fix that. If the consumer can't trust the designer that normal difficulty is balanced, then they're not going to want to keep playing to see if it gets better. The proof of this is in the churn rates of many video games and I have seen games lose more than 50% of their player base within *20 minutes of loading it up*.

One of the best ways to study difficulty in a game is to see how the mechanics hold up on the highest possible setting in the game. This achieves two points:

1. You get to study if the gameplay can hold up when the game is not holding anything back.
2. You can see what the designers define as a challenge in their game.

To that first point, if there are inherent problems with your design, they may end up frustrating or hurting the experience on the lower difficulties and flat out making the game unenjoyable at the higher ones. Due to the reflex-driven nature

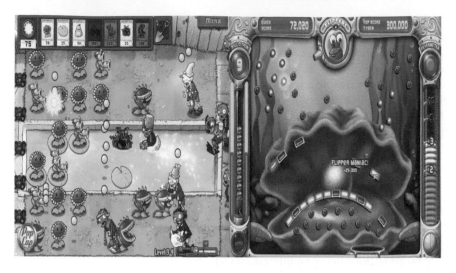

Figure 7.3

At their peak, Popcap Games was one of the premier studios for casual games in the 2000s. Their games were very easy to get into, had hours of entertainment and were designed so that anyone could start playing them.

of action and soulslike games, the consumer can figure out quickly if the game is right for them and if they are enjoying the gameplay.

Depth is not the same as complexity. There have been hundreds, maybe even thousands at this point, of games that are highly complex to play and learn. This includes grand strategy games, management sims, and many cult classics of the 80s–90s. In retrospect, just because these games were hard to learn, didn't mean that they had depth. The most popular reason why these games were complicated was often due to poor UI/UX, and why I harp on it so much now. We can see this in action watching speedrunners of older games and once they know the exact way to play, the entire game becomes simple.

This section has talked about depth when it comes to hard games, but it's also important to mention how it relates to easier games as well. Some of the best casual games released are not about being basic with no gameplay. Instead, they are about being very easy to pick up and start playing, and then the designers make that gameplay as engaging as possible. A great example of this would be *Plants vs. Zombies* by Popcap Games (released in 2009). The creator, George Fan, gave a talk about how he kept iterating on the gameplay and UI/UX to the point that his mother who didn't play games could learn and figure it out. To wit, it is actually very hard to make a streamlined experience and one that is easy to learn. There is a lot going on in terms of the **GUI** and UI/UX of a game like *Plants vs. Zombies* (Figure 7.3).

The mistake you want to avoid as a designer is thinking that both extremes of making a game easy or hard will make your game successful. Either because

7. A Study of Difficulty

you will attract people who don't like the genre of your game by making it easy or because an extreme challenge will get the hardcore people to praise it. To have depth to your design, you first need to figure out what the baseline of your game is about. The baseline is the minimum level of skill and understanding needed to start playing, and it greatly differs based on the design and genre. Once you have that understood, you can then start approaching your gameplay from different angles in terms of making things easier or harder.

Depth and complexity are often conflated, and why many hard-to-learn games have hardcore fans to them – the people who did figure things out and found the great gameplay underneath. But it takes a good designer to do what they can to make the game as approachable as possible and give people the best possible chance of figuring out and then playing their game. With the successes of From Software over the 2010s, part of their growth was trying to make things more accommodating while still providing the challenging gameplay and philosophy they wanted to do. You always want to start from a place of knowing the audience that you are targeting with your design and then look at ways that you can expand that consumer base.

The reason why this matters is that how people consume games has changed over the 2010s. Previously, if you bought a digital game, that's it, it's yours forever. This meant that people had to be 100% sure that they would like a game before giving the developer a sale. Today, any game bought on Steam has a 2-hour, no questions asked, refund policy. If someone dislikes your game for any reason within those 120 minutes, it can be refunded faster than you can say "git gud." This is why in Section 7.3, I'm going to break down how approachability is a major factor in selling games today, no matter what genre you are working in.

Remember this point, it doesn't matter how good/wonderful/deep a game is, if everyone stops playing it within 20 minutes and never sees that.

7.2 Understanding the Souls Skill Curve

A major aspect of figuring out the market and audience of a game is determining the skill floor, skill curve, and skill ceiling of your design. The skill floor represents the basic level of understanding of the genre and its mechanics to start playing. If we're focusing on a platformer, it would be understanding walking and jumping. The skill floor is the genre qualifier that you are marketing your game with. However, part of the increased interest in approachability is trying to make that skill floor far lower and to give more people a chance at learning a game. This is where tutorials, onboarding, guides, etc. come in.

The skill curve is how the complexity and mechanics of a game grow over the course of playing it. You never want to start at a 1/10 in terms of difficulty to then go 10/10. There must be a measured sense of pacing that the player feels like the game is growing alongside their knowledge of it. This is where we also talk about elements like "difficulty spikes" – when the game introduces something far harder than anything that came before it. Often, this is followed by situations

Figure 7.4

Returning to *Sekiro*, the game features a big difficulty spike in the form of Genichiro who is one of the hardest bosses in the game for new players. He is also considered the big test by the game – for people who do manage to beat him, the rest of the game will be easier by comparison, having learned all the mechanics from this battle. For those that couldn't beat him, this is where the game ends for them.

that are far easier than the spike, which means that the hard section didn't even prepare the player for the next encounter (Figure 7.4). What you want to avoid is having a difficulty wall – where a challenge is so high that it causes a good portion of your audience to stop playing the game.

Lastly, the skill ceiling is the maximum level of understanding and skill that will be required to see the game to its end. I phrased it like that because many games have optional post-game content there as a reward and final challenge for the expert players. Nintendo has done this very well with all the 3D *Mario* games – you never need to collect 100% of the items to beat a *Mario* game, but there are reward and bonus levels for those that do. This level of content is not meant for the general consumer, but for people who want to test their mastery that they have built up while playing the game.

What From Software popularized with their games over the 2010s was having a higher-than-normal skill floor. These are games where it was quite possible and easy to die during the tutorial sections and the very first boss. Each one of the game's first boss fights was known to be a difficulty spike for a lot of players, as it was designed to be the test to see if the player understood the game. Returning to the topic at large with difficulty, this is where the misconception about the difficulty of the soulslike genre comes in – that if the opening of the game is hard, then everything else about it is even harder. However, that's not how these games are designed.

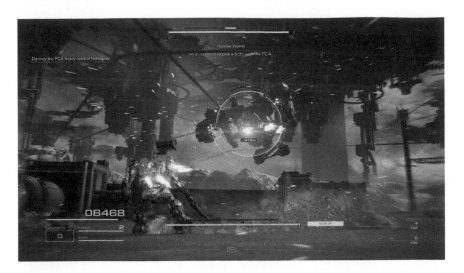

Figure 7.5

At the time of writing this book, *Armored Core 6: Fires of Rubicon* was released by From Software, and its very first boss proved to be a tough wall for a lot of people to get past. Being able to beat it, and understanding how to beat it, will prepare players for the combat system of the game.

Each one of From Software's games released during the 2010s may have started off harder than their contemporaries, but the skill ceiling and skill curve are not as high as other games; action or soulslike included. If you are someone who can beat the first boss of these games, chances are, you are going to be able to go the distance and beat the rest of the game as well. A common trap from other soulslike designers was to keep escalating the combat over the game, increasing the difficulty without giving the player anywhere else to grow. A key aspect of these games is that progression and rewards are often intrinsic – that the player is getting better at the game, and therefore the game is becoming easier. This is again why people who are exceptionally well at these games can do extreme challenge runs. As an interesting point, many of From Software's final bosses for their games are oftentimes easier to beat than the enemies and bosses preceding it. It's not because the bosses' design was made to be purposely easier, but anyone who could reach that fight developed the skills and knowledge needed to beat the game.

The issue that From Software had, and what they've been trying to solve, was to design a game with the pacing and structure to get more people through the learning process and onboarding phase without the need of a boss to beat those lessons in (Figure 7.5). One of my very first game design articles I wrote was about how *Demon's Souls* and the 3D *Mario* games shared similar DNA in terms of their progression and growth. Both games attempted to teach the player how to start playing and then guide them through the advanced elements. *Mario* did this through the design of the levels – offering expert players different routes that were optional but were either quicker or led to bonus rewards. *Demon's Souls* and soulslike did this via boss fights and new enemy patterns. The overall difficulty of both franchises was dependent on the person behind the controller. Every type of player would go through these games in the same way, but the speed and rate of progress were tied to their skill level.

When we turn to *Elden Ring* in Chapter 9, I will talk more about how From Software finally changed their structure and delivered a different kind of pacing and skill curve. As you're designing the progression of your game, you should be trying to figure out what is the overall skill level of the player and the overall power of their character relative to that point in the game. The player is going to use the difficulty and overall threat level of the enemies relative to them to determine what path they should be taking first. It is okay to have an area that is harder than those around it if someone wants to test their skills, but you need to make sure that there is still somewhere to go for people who are still learning the game.

One of the aspects that From Software put into their games was to effectively hide progression systems and functionality at the start of the game. In *Demon's Souls*, the player literally could not level up their character until they managed to beat the first boss of the game, and in *Dark Souls*, upgrading gear required them to get through the tutorial and most of the first official area: Undead Burg. While hiding systems from the player before they are ready for it is a good way of pacing a game, you need to be very mindful of how the game is going to come across for people who aren't as skilled at it. Part of the difficulty problems players had in *Demon's Souls* was the very fact that there was no form of progression available to them until they beat that first stage. If your game is going to be built on a variety of progression and ways of playing, locking players from accessing that at the start may cause frustration.

There is one fundamental lesson about progression that applies to every genre and every kind of player – no one ever wants to feel like they are either stuck or losing progress. An easy way to cause someone to stop playing your game is to take away something they've earned; even if it's just an experience that is easily obtainable again. For the player to feel like they are progressing, there must be some aspect of forward momentum – whether it feels like miles, or millimeters at a time. What has been the major stopping point for people trying to play these games is hitting that proverbial wall – the player can't level up, they can't find any new or better gear, the only option is to beat this fight and move on. When someone becomes stuck at any difficult game, they will do one of two things:

1. They will grit their teeth and keep pushing until they win.
2. They will quit the game and never load it up again (Figure 7.6).

Incidentally, this issue was fixed to some extent with *Elden Ring* and applying open-world design to the soulslike formula. The best kind of skill curve is one where the player feels like the enemies are growing in step with their own

7. A Study of Difficulty

Figure 7.6

Besides loving the look of this enemy from *Nioh*, this was a boss that proved to be frustrating to a lot of people who played it, and by the time I reached it, I was already well acclimated to how the game worked and managed to get through it without dying.

ability – not completely overwhelming them, or the player decimating them. There will always be a bit of a learning curve when fighting a new enemy or entering a new area for the first time, but if you did your job right in terms of onboarding and providing the player with the means of progress, that should not last long.

To that point, part of the difficulty of balancing combat in these games is to avoid making an enemy or boss so difficult that it completely overwhelms all but the most expert portion of your player base. This is why as part of the skill and progression curve of your game, you need to understand that escalation is not the only way to give the player something new. Too many games, not just in the soulslike genre, will continually up the difficulty and complexity in each area. With your skill ceiling, you want to make sure that it's still doable for what is considered the core audience of your game. As I'll talk about in the next chapter with level and environmental design, introducing something that is "new" and not necessarily "harder" can still provide the player with that sense of progression.

When we examine fan mods and fan games of successful franchises, they are most often designed for those fans, AKA: the expert player base. Meaning that to be able to have a remote chance of playing them, you already need to be a master at the base game, and this is why a lot of these fan-made content, no matter how amazing and original they may be, will never be enjoyed by most of the overall fan base. For the designer, it is fine to let people create expert content like that, but as I said earlier, you should never be balancing your skill curve just for your expert players.

Designing the flow of your game is about providing every player with content that they can handle without punishing people for either being too good or too bad at it. For expert players, they don't want to be forced to do content below their skill level, and novice players shouldn't be thrown into the deep end. However, when you are designing a game meant to provide a challenge, that also means accepting that you are going to be limiting your consumer base to some extent. If someone cannot or refuses to meet the skill floor of your game, then that will be a lost player. It is a tough line to walk as a designer, and why From Software's games remained niche until *Demon's Souls*. There are ways to help someone learn a game or provide features to make it easier, but if it comes at the expense of upsetting your core gameplay loop or ruining the balance of your game, then you risk alienating your fanbase who have come to play your game for that specific gameplay.

This is why you need to understand what makes something easy or hard and not just change stats hoping that it will make your game easier or harder. If your game was fixed because you adjusted stats, then that means that you failed when it came to balancing your design. And even then, stat adjustment will not fix any underlying issues with your gameplay. I've played action games that have received balance patches that tried to make things easier without adjusting the problems people had with the game. What happened was that it annoyed the hardcore fans who felt that the designers were removing the challenge, but it didn't fix the underlying problems that kept novices and core players from enjoying it. And that takes us to what approachability means for any game, and why it is essential to learn.

7.3 Why Approachability Matters

Part of understanding the philosophy that goes with difficulty design is being able to distinguish what aspects of your game should be difficult or challenging and what parts should *never* be difficult. A trend of the 2010s in terms of game design was taking a closer look at accessibility and approachability in games, large and small. Thanks to organizations like AbleGamers, there has been a greater call for making games easier to play. However, there are people who argue against this and where the opinion that difficulty equals quality has come from.

The fundamental aspect of developing a game as a designer is understanding who the core audience of your game is – is it casual puzzle fans? Hardcore FPS, middle-of-the-road platformers, and the list goes on (Figure 7.7). Once you've established that audience, that is who you are going to build your core gameplay loop around and set up your skill floor, curve, and ceiling toward. However, that doesn't mean you are done with the presentation of your game. I'll talk more about the UI/UX in Section 8.5, but part of building a good UX is providing approachability and accessibility options in your game.

A lot of people conflate the two terms, and every approachability option is an example of accessibility, but not every accessibility option is also an approachable one. In my opinion, we can define the two features as such:

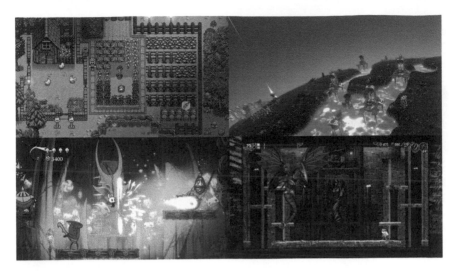

Figure 7.7

Casual or hardcore, mainstream or niche, no matter what kind of game you are building, you need to understand that there will be people who are masters at the genre, and those to whom this will be their very first exposure playing your game. Part of understanding and building your game to be approachable is to make sure that anyone picking it up can start learning how to play it. Indie developers had to learn this as the market blew up in the 2010s and many are still working on it.

Accessibility – Options or features that allow someone to be able to play a game who has a specific condition or outside factor, that is interfering with it.

Approachability – Options or features that make the gameplay easier for everyone.

With those definitions, accessibility features would include, but is not limited to, colorblind mode, subtitles, reducing or removing physically strenuous elements, disabling photosensitive scenes, and much more. In this respect, accessibility options allow more people to play a game who would otherwise not be able to play or experience it as well due to their own ability or condition. To learn more about accessibility features and ways of improving your game, you can visit the IGDA Accessibility SIG[1] and AbleGamers. There is no reason for any game to purposely ignore or be designed against accessibility options in today's market. Not only that but including elements that are anti-accessible is a sure way to hurt your game's marketability.

When we discuss approachability, these are elements that improve the overall playability of a game but are not necessarily about adding or changing said gameplay. Most approachability options fall under the banner of quality of life or QOL features. The goal of approachability features is to remove, or mitigate as much as

Figure 7.8

One genre that has seen some of the biggest moves for approachability in the 2010s to today is the fighting game. Fighting games are notoriously difficult for new players to get into and enjoy, and a lot of work major franchises have done has been trying to make them easier to learn and provide content for non-hardcore players to enjoy. *Street Fighter 6* by Capcom on the left features an optional "modern" control scheme that reduces complexity, and *Mortal Kombat 1* by NetherRealm Studios has an expanded single-player story and bonus content for people who don't want to fight other players, along with extensive tutorial features (both released in 2023).

possible, any pain points or elements that distract from the core gameplay loop. Here, approachability is used to allow more people to enjoy a game who may not have the same skill level or tolerance for difficulty or pain points that hardcore fans would have (Figure 7.8). That last point is important because while your hardcore fans are often the loudest and most supportive of your game, they are usually not the best group to ask about approachability features. The reason is that they are the group that has internalized any issues or problems within your game as part of the experience, hence why this group is the one that will say "git gud" when people argue about approachability and balancing.

As a designer, it's important to understand what aspects of your game are meant to be challenging. Anything that revolves around onboarding, UI/UX, or systems not related to the core gameplay of a title should not be difficult to understand or utilize. There are many RPGs and mobile games that feature extensive side systems of progression, currency, upgrading, etc., that often are there to give the impression that the game is deep, but are just meant to be confusing. Anytime the player has to stop playing your game to look something up, consult a guide, or is otherwise not engaging with the core gameplay loop, that is an area that you need to look at in terms of approachability and UX.

7. A Study of Difficulty

Approachability and UI/UX mean different things for real-time or turn-based games, and if I tackle aspects of the strategy genre in a future Deep Dive, I will cover the latter there. For real-time games, a lot of the work done in terms of approachability is about providing as much clarity to the player as possible on what is happening at any given time and keeping them in the action. Features like auto-equipping gear, quick-use slots for items, and an easy-to-follow menu system are just some of the major ones. With soulslikes, one particular focus has been making the act of leveling and applying stat points as easy as possible. Today, these games will explain as clearly as they can what each attribute will do, what they will impact, and how much. Being able to easily sort through items and equipment of different types can be very important in soulslikes, as it can be difficult sometimes to remember what an item was while the player is picking up a lot of things in an area.

I'll discuss more about the GUI and UI in Section 8.5, but it's important to understand that the role of approachability is that the player should always be engaging with the core gameplay loop. Anytime they must switch to another screen to do something, that needs to be as painless as possible. Approachability and QOL features aren't going to make a bad game great, but they are often the death-by-a-thousand cuts reasons why people will stop playing a game. As I mentioned earlier, thanks to Steam's refund policy, consumers don't need a lot of excuses to refund a game they're not enjoying.

One other aspect of approachability and accessibility that has been debated is the use of "assist modes." An assist mode is a feature that effectively allows the player to bypass difficult content without the need to play it. While this is a useful feature, I would debate not necessarily calling it an approachability option, as the intended purpose is to skip playing through the game. This is a feature that has obvious positives and negatives associated with it. Having one in your game can almost guarantee that people will be able to get through it. However, balancing, or ignoring to balance your game under the assumption that people can just use it is a horrible idea. This goes back to the overall purpose of approachability features – *they are not there to fix your game or ignore problems but to make what's there better* (Figure 7.9). If testers are complaining about a system or a particular area in your game, putting in the option to just skip it doesn't remove those complaints. Think of assist modes like an airbag in a car – an option that must be there but should only be used if there is an absolute emergency. The very worst thing you can do to your game with this is to knowingly have something that people don't like or complain about and still include it with the option to turn it off.

However, there is a major advantage to assist modes when they are used to make a game more accessible to a larger market. A big example of this comes from the survival genre, where it is possible to disable certain elements that increase difficulty – removing the failure state of dying of thirst, having a free play or sandbox mode, and even allowing the player to manually tweak various aspects of the design. The reason why this works is that survival games tend to

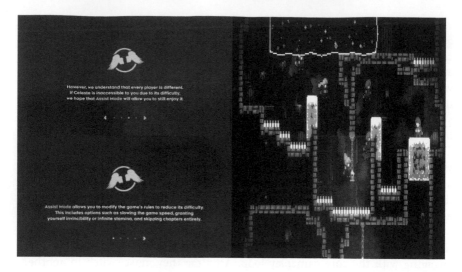

Figure 7.9

Celeste (released in 2018 by Maddy Makes Games Inc.) was one of the first games to feature assist mode options. The game is one of the most challenging 2D platformers commercially released, but the assist modes allow anyone to be able to play the game all the way through. While there is the standard experience as the developers intended, these options open the game up to more people without affecting those who will not use them.

have a creative component to them with building structures, homes, castles, etc. that are separate from the other gameplay loops. By being able to turn off fail states, it allows the audience who wants to engage with the building to be able to enjoy it fully. And like the *Celeste* example mentioned above, if someone wants the challenge and difficulty, then they can play the game that way. For soulslikes, which are by their nature very button-heavy to play, I could see the case to implement options that could slow down the game, make some of the more advanced maneuvers easier to do, and other details. While purists have complained about having these options, in a single-player game, there is no need to worry about how someone else is experiencing a game. I even created a list of approachability options that I felt could work with any soulslike design.[2]

Before you can start thinking about approachability options and UX in your game, you first need to establish and set what the baseline experience of your game will be. The baseline is both the intended experience and the most approachable version of it. Once that is decided and set, then it is possible to start looking at ways of making that easier or have elements to add difficulty and challenge to your game if people want it. In *Game Design Deep Dive: Roguelikes*, I spoke about progressive difficulty options – ways that the player can decide to make the game harder if they choose. It is far easier to convince someone to try to make the game more challenging with options than it is to have them turn something off or reduce the difficulty. This goes with the baseline – if you tell someone that "normal" is your intended difficulty, then they are going to expect everything in that to be balanced and enjoyable. If they are not enjoying "normal", the general player is not going to start looking at assist modes or other options to try and fix things; they are going to quit the game. If they enjoy what the normal experience of the game is, but want to then make things easier or harder, having those options in place will allow them to finetune their play. With the survival game example mentioned above, approachability options and assist modes work because the market for these games includes two audiences – people who want to survive, and those who want to build.

The overall mission statement for this chapter is to get you to start thinking about how difficulty and challenge will work in your game. What makes souslikes very hard to do right is creating a balanced, and still challenging, gameplay experience. The people who are attracted to these games are like the fighting game genre – they want complete control over whether they succeed. Before you can start looking at improving the approachability of your game, you need to establish the baseline experience as I went over in the last paragraph, and what your skill floor is going to be. From there, it is then possible to examine where people are having trouble with your game and can then take steps to mitigate them. Some of the best approachability options are those that are inherently or explicitly optional. Inherent would be providing different routes and playstyles for your audience. Explicitly would be having toggleable options that change your game to make it easier or harder.

And one final point about approachability, the player needs to know that approachability options exist in your game. Even if that means literally coming out and telling them right at the start (Figure 7.10). Too many indie games I've played have had issues with their gameplay that were fixed in the assist mode but said assist mode could be three or four screens deep within the menu. Another route is to have the option pop up in the game if the player is stuck at a section to let them know that they could make things easier.

There is no perfect list of approachability options for video games, as every genre is different. You need to listen to the player base, and even to those outside of it if you want to improve the approachability and playability. If you can make your game enjoyable and approachable for the soulslike master who understands every aspect of the design and will crush your game, and the novice who will use options like "auto-healing" and slowing down combat, then you are off to a great start.

7.4 What People Get Wrong about Soulslikes

In my book *Game Design Deep Dive: Roguelikes* I talked about where a lot of critics of the genre often misunderstand the point of the gameplay, and there are similar aspects of that with soulslikes. Throughout this chapter, my goal was to try and expand on the concept of difficulty and depth. As I said earlier, many

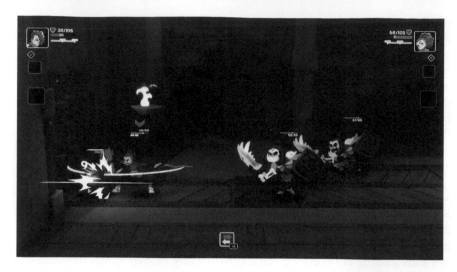

Figure 7.10

Young Souls (released in 2022 by 1P2P) was a game that I played through but had issues with the general feel of the combat. What I discovered after having a frustrating time was that there were assist features available to remove those pain points. I can guarantee for you reading this that most people who stopped playing the game did not even know that there were assist features available, because the game didn't have any indication that they were there.

people conflate difficulty as the major takeaway to the success of *Dark Souls*, both fans and critics alike. While these games are challenging, the best ones, specifically the ones by From Software, are not meant to be overly hard (Figure 7.11). With roguelike design, many critics view it as just unbridled chaos where the player has no control over whether they win or lose. And while there are some roguelikes that go that far, good designers create experiences that are meant to reward the player who learns it.

I can guarantee every one of you reading this book right now that most of the people who argue that all soulslikes are too difficult to learn never reached a quarter of the way through these games. The reason why I know this is because good soulslikes become easier to play the further someone gets. Again, there are fewer examples that keep escalating the difficulty to the point that it becomes a problem. The reason why From Software became the benchmark for the subgenre has been their approach and design, and it comes from one simple principle – learning through failure.

In an interview Miyazaki gave to the New Yorker in 2022,[3] he spoke about wanting the player to find purpose in failure. This is very much the same kind of mantra we see from the roguelike genre – there is not one player who has ever beaten a roguelike on their very first play. What makes soulslikes and roguelikes similar is that the player is being taught two things at the same time – how to play

Figure 7.11

Elden Ring's success surprised a lot of designers who felt that the whole souls-like design was too hard and demanding for people to play. However, it was the most approachable soulslike from the studio, and along with the prestige of From Software's name, became the most successful game released in 2022.

the game and how the rules of the game work. Every From Software soulslike gives the player an overview of all the major aspects of the gameplay, but then leaves it up to the player to put it all together within the rules of the world.

> "We are always looking to improve, but, in our games specifically, hardship is what gives meaning to the experience. So, it's not something we're willing to abandon at the moment. It's our identity." - Hidetaka Miyazaki

I also want to make something very clear; ***failure is not the same as punishment***. If someone is so focused on the punishment, they're never going to take a risk or try and learn something. There is a reason why the only thing that the player loses in these games is their experience, even though it is obviously important, it is replaceable. Anyone who has played these games knows that at some point you stop caring about the souls you lose, and instead focus on the challenge at hand. Punishment creates "weight" to the experience – that the player isn't just losing time, but they are being set back further. The problem with punishment in this respect is that it only impacts the players who are having trouble with the game and don't need anything more to happen. The faster that someone can get back to attempting what they were doing, the better the experience will be. Returning to the previous section, this is why letting the player make things harder is preferable to just forcing those options onto someone who doesn't need/want them.

In the next chapter, I'm going to focus on the design and how as the designer you are going to attempt to motivate the player through failure. The thrill of

Figure 7.12

The opening of a From Software game tends to be one of the hardest sections in the game, not because they are designed to be hard, but because they expect a lot out of the player from the word "go." It is often why the first boss of their games is either meant to teach the player how to play or introduce them to the fact that death and failure are always around the corner.

soulslikes and what drives people to play them is the intrinsic reward of overcoming a challenge and the extrinsic reward of making permanent progress. What is often the stumbling block for new players is that very notion that you are being set up to fail from the very first second of starting the game (Figure 7.12). This could also be the reason why several of From Software's soulslikes literally start with an event that kills the player.

Unfortunately, here is the major problem with this philosophy, and one that Miyazaki knows all too well – a lot of people don't like learning through losing. One of the repeated arguments against these games is that video games are supposed to be relaxing and not something that is a struggle to play. For people like me, and I'm going to assume fans of these games, the focus and demanding nature are what makes them so relaxing for us. The point that has been drilled in by From Software is that these games are about 100% focus on the player's part; anything less than that and they are going to lose. Incidentally, we have seen other soulslikes that tried to be far easier to play, and they did not resonate with this specific audience.

And this is the reason why for you reading this, soulslikes are going to remain a niche genre; even with the massive success of *Elden Ring*. To do a soulslike right, you are inherently going to be making a game that is not for everyone. But that does not mean actively ignoring UI/UX conventions, and approachability and accessibility features. There is a massive difference between someone who

Figure 7.13

Games that have high skill floors and ceiling will attract people who only want things to be as difficult and as challenging as possible. With *Doom Eternal*'s DLC episodes, they were far harder to play than the base game and introduced new elements to add to the challenge. However, it led to a split in the community among those who wanted harder challenges seen in the first DLC, or more different challenges seen in the second.

refuses to learn a soulslike because they hate challenge and learning through failure, and someone who wants to play these games but is physically incapable of manipulating the controls at the required speed. I interviewed Stephen Spohn from AbleGamers,[4] and he made a fantastic point on the nature of accessibility and approachability options in difficult games. He said that for someone like me, I want a challenging game and I can play these games at their normal speed and enjoy them for that level of challenge. For someone like him, he also wants to play a challenging game, but he would get the same thrill that I would get if he could play that game at half speed or even slower.

The final point I want to make in this section is that playing hard games requires a give-and-take between the designers and the audience. The audience must be ready for an experience that is going to challenge them, and the designers need to understand the balancing and pacing to create an engaging experience. As I said in Section 7.1, creating a challenging and rewarding experience is not the same as just making a difficult one; no matter how many hardcore fans say otherwise (Figure 7.13). If someone is willing to make that nonverbal agreement to be challenged by your game, then it is on you to create a well-designed and balanced game that doesn't feel like you are just punishing the player. There is a fine line between making something that is a challenge and making something that is difficult because of mistakes or issues in your gameplay, and that takes understanding the finer points of this design.

Notes

1 https://igda-gasig.org/
2 https://medium.com/super-jump/can-approachability-fix-dark-souls-29268917fc3
3 https://www.newyorker.com/culture/persons-of-interest/hidetaka-miyazaki-sees-death-as-a-feature-not-a-bug
4 https://game-wisdom.com/videos/ablegamers-accessibility-games

8

Advanced Soulslike Design

8.1 What Is Level and Environmental Design?

For any action-based game that involves exploring, it is crucial that you understand what level and environmental design mean to a game. When we talk about level design, this is focusing on the elements that are actively challenging the player in any given area – where are enemies going to be set up? What are the hazards in the area? Where are the shortcuts and rest areas?

Environmental design is about the **aesthetics** of the area – what does this place look like? What kind of architecture and foliage make up the space? What is the story of this location?

The overall world design of each of From Software's games has always received high praise from fans and reviewers, as they manage to combine both level and environmental design almost seamlessly into one, but understanding the design of these games requires you to view them at first as two separate entities (Figure 8.1).

For a more practical example of the difference between the two, I'm going to talk about the same area in two ways: from an environmental design view and then from a level design.

DOI: 10.1201/9781003450078-8

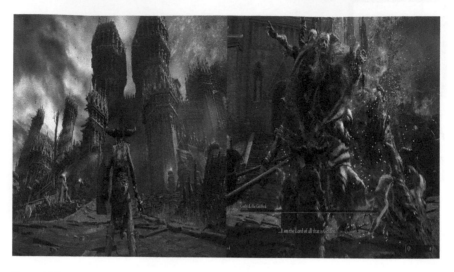

Figure 8.1

Level and environmental design are two sides of the coin when you are building the world of your game. Here, Stormveil Castle from *Elden Ring* is designed to be the game's first "level" players will explore, with Godrick on the right as the first Elden lord waiting for players at the end.

Environmental – Suspended in air by powerful wind currents over a volcano, a massive castle ominously blocks out the sun. The only way to approach it is by climbing up chains connected to the top of the volcano while guards on smaller platforms guard against any attack. For anyone who can get past the guards at the front gate, they will find a massive courtyard with lava flowing all around used to power the various machines. A giant tower looms over the courtyard where the king of the castle is holed up.

Level – The player will start the area at the top of the volcano where they must fight two basic swordsmen who are guarding the chain. Near the chain will be a wooden support base with a rope that appears to go straight to the front gate of the castle. Running up the chain, the player will have to deal with flying gargoyles who throw spears at them before arriving at the first platform. The platform will have three swordsmen and one commander that the player must fight or run past to reach the second platform. This platform is larger and will have two swords-men, four archers, and two commanders guarding it. Reach the top of the chain, and there will be a mini boss of a grand gargoyle. Defeating the enemy will open the front gate and give access to the courtyard. There will be a small guard post to the side of the main gate that the player can find where they can activate a platform that will bypass the chain climbing that connects from the wooden base back up to the castle gate.

There is a lot more detail I could go into, but you should have the point. Whether you think about your game from an environmental or a level design

8. Advanced Soulslike Design

point of view first depends on the kind of designer you are. If you are more story-driven, then you'll probably come up with the kind of world you want the game to take place in first. For designers looking at creating a challenge, they will be thinking about the level design first.

In terms of what is more important to the game because we are talking about a reflex-driven genre, level design, or specifically, great level design, is more important. If your game is not good from a level design standpoint, then that is going to affect how combat plays out, how the pacing of your game is structured, and can lead to people getting lost, frustrated, and bored with it.

However, not thinking about environmental design can leave you with a world that is very static and flat to explore. This is often the weakness seen in other soulslikes, where every room looks like the previous, and there is no structure to the environment. As I said earlier in the book, many action games treated their levels purely from a level design standpoint, creating rooms that simply served as space to fight enemies and nothing more. Part of environmental design is that the environments should feel like they exist within the world itself. That means not only designing interesting obstacles and challenges, but creating unique landmarks and a space that guides the player through it. As I said further up, one of the key aspects of From Software's success in this space is the merging of both forms of design. Not only does every area stand out with its own look and feel, but that extends into the level design itself, and that is something you should be paying attention to. A good area from a level design standpoint needs to feel original; have a proper beginning, middle, and end to it; and it needs to feel like the challenges of the level match the environment that it takes place in (Figure 8.2).

Let us talk about Blighttown from *Dark Souls 1*, as it is one of the most memorable areas in the series for being an absolute pain to explore. It is one of the few vertical levels in the entire series. From an environmental perspective, the story is that the town itself is a massive shanty town built for the poor and lower-class workers. The as-for-mentioned blight has infected everyone and comes from the very floor of the area itself. From a level design standpoint, players will either start at the very top or access the town at the halfway point from a shortcut. Most paths are very narrow making it easy to fall and die while fighting enemies. Besides the mutated villagers, there are giant bugs to deal with. The area features several hard sections that have led to many character deaths. There are villagers using blowguns to inflict the toxic status, which is a more powerful form of poison. Before the player reaches the bottom, they need to time landing on platforms that run on a water mill-like conveyor and ride it down to the floor. At the floor, the player's character will be constantly exposed to poison while dodging brutes that throw rocks at them and head toward a massive cocoon to fight the area boss. There is more to this area in terms of items found and secrets, but this is the general structure that every player must deal with and I do mean literally every player. This is because Blighttown represents the end of the first quarter of the game – it is required to be beaten to unlock the area known as Sen's Fortress which will then take the player into the next section of the game.

Figure 8.2

The Undead Settlement is considered the second major area in *Dark Souls 3*, with the theme that you are fighting through the remains of a village. The bulk of the enemies are undead villagers who stand in your way of reaching the area boss: a giant living tree.

When we examine proficient level design in any genre, it's important to view a level as a cohesive whole made up of individualized sections. This is at its purest with the platformer genre. The actual level will have a theme or mission statement that runs through it, and each section will represent a different part of said theme. When describing a "section", this can be as short or as long as the designer intended, but there are often clear signs when the player moves from one section to another. This can be in the form of a checkpoint that exists between the two, a noticeable change in the environment or enemies, or as something as simple as moving from one screen to another in older games.

A checkpoint refers to something that marks the player's progress and removes the need to replay the previous area. In soulslikes, checkpoints come in the form of opening shortcuts and finding new rest areas. With older titles, checkpoints occur after a section is over, but due to the size of soulslikes, checkpoints are often hard fought. This is where the risk/reward that is a huge aspect of these games come in – the player must weigh either returning to the last checkpoint to restock and bank their experience or keep pushing forward to try and make actual progress (Figure 8.3).

Returning to the theme, this represents the sum of the aesthetics and the challenge that you want to test the player with. Good level design is about settling on one theme per area and making that as focused as possible. It is better to design

8. Advanced Soulslike Design

Figure 8.3

The thrill of Soulslike design is the act of making permanent progress in the game. Just reaching a bonfire, or bonfire analog, gives the player the knowledge that the part of the game they were in is now complete, and they can start focusing on the next area. Good level design also means understanding how far and how many checkpoints like this you want in a single level.

three smaller levels each with a focused theme, as opposed to one large and unfocused level. Another aspect of a good theme and good design is understanding how this relates to difficulty. As I said earlier in the book, there are designers who felt that the only way to design new content in a soulslike, or any action-driven game, is via escalation – just keep making it harder and harder. Good designers understand that difficulty is just one of the ways to create new content; the other is to focus on unique sections that test the player's skills in different ways. You should treat your theme as a template, and then, look for all ways of expressing it through your environmental and level design. To use *Dark Souls* as an example, the area after Sen's Fortress is known as Anor Londo; it is a massive cityscape where the player must run across narrow beams and bridges, and fight their way to the main castle. The theme is a very wide spacious environment punctuated with many paths that the player can be hit off and fall to their death.

I want to clarify one point in case a few of you reading this may have not picked up on it; even though soulslikes and most action games today don't technically follow the same stage format that classic games did, they are still technically set up around that framing. Most soulslikes are built on the following types of environments:

1. The Hub/Homebase – an area where the player is safe from harm and where essential vendors are located.
2. Transitionary Areas – locations that simply serve as the connection between two or more other places the player must reach.
3. The Stage itself – an area that the player must completely explore with an established beginning, middle, and boss to fight at the end.

In *Dark Souls 1*, Firelink Shrine acts as the game's hub, with the area growing with more characters as the player completes quests. The Valley of Drakes is a transitionary area that is mainly used as a shortcut to get to the halfway point in Blighttown, but also connects to New Londo Ruins and Darkroot Garden. Transitionary areas may have a boss fight in it, but it is not required to defeat it and can be avoided if need be.

For the stage example, I want to go into more detail about Sen's Fortress, because this level is the perfect encapsulation of the focus on sections and theme from the first *Dark Souls*. Let's start with the actual route the player is going to take, and I'm going to organize this in terms of sections:

1. The player goes through the front door and is attacked by two snake guards.
2. The next room is a run across a narrow platform with blades swinging like a pendulum. There is a shortcut here to the top of the area that is inaccessible when the player first gets here. After running across and beating the enemy, they must go upstairs to another bridge with more blades and a spell-throwing snake man.
3. After a small room that connects to several hidden areas, the player comes to a large room with a narrow passageway. Boulders are being thrown down that the character must duck into holes in the wall to avoid. At the top is a spiral passageway. Going up, they can find the boulder launcher and redirect it to uncover secrets. Running down will take the character deeper into the fortress.
4. The player enters a room where a treasure chest turns out to be a mimic that they can fight for a reward; taking an elevator up, they will arrive at more bridges with swinging blades, snakemen, and traps to avoid. Getting past this will take them to the top of the fortress.
5. Along the top of the fortress, the player can see a giant who is responsible for throwing boulders down in Section 3 and another one that will toss exploding bombs at them as they approach. They can also find a bonfire that is the first and only checkpoint in this stage. There are large and elite knights to get past and a second giant. Running across narrow ledges will take them into a central tower. If the player finds a cage key and opens up a cage and gets into it, they will discover that this is a shortcut back to Section 2. At the top of this area, they will find a fog door that leads to the boss: The Iron Golem.

What I just described is the general layout and pathing of the stage, not considering the optional and secret areas that make up Sen's Fortress. You can see with this layout how we can break down each individual section of the stage, while the theme is that of a trap-filled fortress. To simplify things further, the stage could also be split simply into two sections – the lower area and the upper one – but that doesn't give as clear of a breakdown.

To understand this kind of sectional design in a soulslike, as you're playing through a stage, take note of any time when the level design introduces a change: a new environment, a new kind of obstacle, or a new enemy. Those are examples of a change in the sections. You should also pay attention to any shortcuts set up and what sections do they allow the player to bypass. Based on the difficulty and length of the overall stage, there may be multiple shortcuts that bypass different amounts of content, and a major one that acts as the shortcut from the bonfire directly to the boss at the end. Any time there is a checkpoint, note how many sections the player had to go through to reach it. Difficulty in terms of level design is twofold – how hard is each individualized section, and how far are shortcuts and checkpoints spaced out? In the last chapter, I brought up the concept of weight and how it can be used as a form of punishment. The more sections someone must repeat, if they die, will add to frustration. If you want to make things easier for the player, you can have checkpoints or shortcuts set up before and after a very difficult section. This allows someone to instantly restart and not have to repeat it once they get past it once.

You can have a hard level in any game made a lot easier if there are plenty of checkpoints that prevent the player from losing any time if they fail a section. In some platformers I've played, there may be multiple checkpoints within a single section to remove any punishment when the player fails (Figure 8.4).

Returning to environmental design, the environment and the aesthetics of the stage should still adhere to the theme, even if the player enters new locations within the stage. Some games will use an exception to this rule and have the environment completely changed to signal a major progression point within the stage itself. In New Londo Ruins from *Dark Souls 1*, the stage starts out with the area completely submerged in water that is lethal to the character. If they can reach about the halfway point of the stage, they can activate the gate that leads out to the Valley of Drakes and drain most of the water. From that point forward, the player can jump down from the ledges to the drained areas as both a shortcut and route to the back half of the stage and where the boss fight is located.

Environmental hazards can mean just about anything to the level design of a game. Part of building the level design is about how the level itself, separate from enemies, will challenge the player. This could include traps that shoot blow darts, floors that give way when stepped on, and even literally dropping a boulder on someone for stepping on the wrong tile. The severity of the hazard needs to be weighed with how apparent it is in the environment. A classic example of frustrating design in games was plenty of role-playing games (RPGs) and roguelikes in the 80s that featured literal death traps – the player triggers them, they

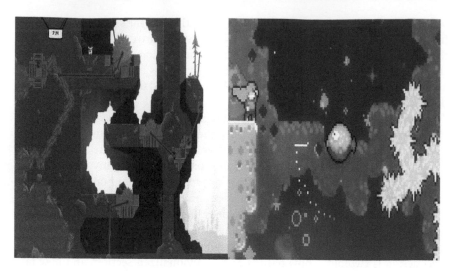

Figure 8.4

Challenging platformers such as *Super Meat Boy* (released in 2010 by Team Meat) used shorter levels to balance out the difficulty of the game, with many levels taking less than a minute, or even 30 seconds to clear. With *Celeste* mentioned earlier, the game checkpoints after every section, but the length and complexity of them grew as the game went on.

automatically die. With these traps, there was no way to spot them until it was too late, with many adventure games having similar fail states that were put in to sell strategy guides and hint lines. While it's okay to have a trap that is hard to spot, you don't want to put into an already challenging game something that can kill the player without any warning or tell before the fact. An exception to this rule is if you use the death to introduce a new concept or standard going forward that can slip up the player if they're not careful. Perhaps one of the most famous examples of *Dark Souls* was the introduction of "the mimic". An enemy that appears just like any of the treasure chests in the game, but can appear slightly discolored or twitch slightly to indicate that something is not right. If the player tries to open the mimic, it will grab them and either kill them or do a lot of damage.

Be aware that if you want to have challenges that require specific physical maneuvers, like dodging, rolling, jumping, and so on, the game's user interface (UI) must be set up to make those aspects easy to perform. One of the major differences between earlier soulslikes by From Software, and what they did with *Elden Ring*, was to have far more platforming and jumping obstacles in *Elden Ring*. The reason why this worked was *Elden Ring* made jumping a core mechanic to the game and made it easy to do as part of the UI. Previous games where jumping wasn't important required the player to either push the analog stick in (or known as L3/R3) or double-tap the dodge button while running to perform a

Figure 8.5

The Divine Tower of Caelid is an area that would have never been doable in the earlier soulslikes when jumping was not a primary mechanic. This entire area requires the player to first climb up from the outside, then work their way down inside of it, with any missteps leading to a deadly fall. Despite not designing their games around jumping in the past, From Software did an excellent job of designing levels around it with *Elden Ring*.

jump. It was very awkward to pull off and was only used by the level design when hiding secrets and not on the main path (Figure 8.5).

Another facet of environmental design is using the environment itself to "guide" the player through the level. An implicit example would be having a major landmark way in the distance that the player must head to. Many designers use explicit ways of guiding the player – having one lamppost shining on a door, using fences and debris to block inaccessible areas, and more. This is important for games that take place in enclosed spaces, where the player can't see as far out into the distance. There needs to be notable landmarks that the player can use to guide themselves around. If every room looks the same or has the same general tone to it, then it becomes easy to get lost.

There is one other point to be made about level design with the use of procedural generation or procgen. Procedural generation can be used in two ways when building the level and environmental design of a title. The first is literally having the game generate all content, all level design, and all pathing from beginning to end. This is the kind of procgen that has famously been a part of the roguelike genre and its subgenres. The second kind of procgen occurs during development of the game, and this is where the designers will generate the environment's basic topography of the world before manually editing and adding in the levels and level design of the game.

Good soulslike level design is about giving the individualized levels them-selves personality and depth to them, and that is something that procgen is not able to do well. The reason why it works with roguelike design is that roguelike levels are meant to be replayed, with the rewards and structure different in each play. The focus of a roguelike is on how the player is progressing and growing in power differently on each run. Soulslikes are meant to have a specific path and progression through them. Once the player clears an entire stage, they're not meant to replay it each time after their character dies. Returning to *Bloodborne*, while the chalice dungeons did provide rewards for going through them, there was little to no personality to each one, with the only defining moments being boss fights. *Remnant: From the Ashes* had the same problem – without providing variance on each play, shuffling up the order of the worlds or moving around map elements did not change what the player was doing. The only things that mat-tered were what points of interest showed up and the bosses they would fight. The issue that procgen has is that the game is dealing with hardcoded elements and hazards defined by the developers. No matter how those elements are shuffled and rearranged, this does not change how they are dealt with. If the player only has one way of dealing with a spinning blade trap, then it doesn't matter where it shows up if the player's option is the same each time. You simply cannot instill personality into a level through procgen the same way that a designer can build it from scratch. It can be used to generate the topography, and then create the individualized levels that exist in that space, such as in *Elden Ring's* case.

Good level design is all about that sense of "personality" – that the area not only provides a suitable challenge, but it makes sense within the world and stands out from the other areas (Figure 8.6). Making sure that the beginning, middle, and end all work is a lot harder than it sounds, and many games have failed to stick the landing of their levels. And that takes me to a hard question to answer: what is a bad level in this respect? There are several details that we can see in games where the level and environmental design don't work. From a level standpoint, if a level is too long or frustrating to navigate, it can easily wear on a player's nerves. Speaking from the environmental standpoint, you want to avoid areas that lack any sense of personality to them – such as just having the same kind of room copied and pasted repeatedly. This is also why designing stages that take place inside a structure are harder to make stand out. When you're inside a building, your vision is obviously limited based on the walls and the room you're in. It becomes harder to make a mental map of an area if you are only able to see things one room at a time. Outside, you have far greater vision and can put together the layout of the area far easier.

You should also be mindful of designing levels with graphical effects that can become obnoxious to deal with. In the original *Dark Souls*, two of the later levels were nightmares to navigate due to different uses of lighting. In the Lost Izalith, the bloom, or lighting, of the lava was so bright in areas that it drowned out the ability for the player to properly see what was going on. In the area the Tomb of the Giants, there is little to no visibility, with the player surrounded by many

Figure 8.6

From Software's art direction has yet to be matched by any other soulslike studio in delivering areas that all look fantastic, stand out from one another, and fit within the structure of their world. *Elden Ring* was highly praised for its design and look, and these are just a snippet of the variety of areas players will explore in the game.

bottomless pits. The only way to navigate is by bringing an external light source, but even then, the player's visibility is only a few feet ahead of them. Low lighting and visibility in games can also cause eye strain and can lead to people developing headaches or migraines if they are playing for too long, which has happened to me on several occasions. Those last two examples bring up an important point, a level that feels annoying to play due to its constraints or rules may have personality to it, but it will be remembered not as fondly as the rest of the game. Be aware of how technical limitations can affect how someone plays through a stage. Elements like slowdown and disorienting visuals can occur. If you can't figure out how to stop them from happening, you may need to redesign stages or come up with a clever solution to mitigate them. As an interesting example, *Dark Souls* 1–3 would feature areas where the player must ride an inordinately long elevator or lift. These areas give the game time to load and render the next area without having to stop the game for a loading screen. They also provide the means of allowing areas to connect to each other without having to design them in a way that would require the game to be rendering two or more full areas at the same time.

This section does not begin to explain the difficulty that goes into designing a great and memorable stage, let alone for the soulslike genre. Just remember that like everything else with soulslike design, quality is better than quantity. You need to justify the existence of each stage – how does it stand out from the other stages? What unique tests and challenges will it have? How does it relate to the rest of the world? If you can't answer those points when deciding whether to cut a stage from your game, then you may already have your answer.

8.2 Reflex-Driven Enemy Design

The last time in the Deep Dive series I talked about enemy design was on the horror genre. Soulslikes, and extending to action-based design, have a greater focus on the enemies and how they are balanced compared to other genres. In my RPG book, I spoke about enemy design strictly on the nature of the skills and abilities they can use, but we now need to focus on what this means in a real-time environment. Sections 8.2 and 8.3 are extensions of what I began to lay out in Chapter 3.

What separates enemy design in soulslikes from traditional action games is their purpose. In most reflex-driven games, enemies are designed to be nothing more than a brief obstacle – something for the player to destroy and show off while doing it. This has also led to several games that turn the act of killing enemies into score chasing or rewarding the player for how stylish they are while fighting – with the *Devil May Cry* series by Capcom one of the standout examples. When there are harder enemies to fight, like bosses, they still don't provide that much of a threat to someone who knows how to play the game.

What From Software did was change how action games approach designing enemies and turn them into legitimate threats against the player (Figure 8.7). This kind of enemy design was first used in the *Monster Hunter* series by Capcom

Figure 8.7

Big or small, animal or humanoid, there is no limit to creating interesting enemies, and all of From Software's soulslikes feature a memorable selection to go against the players, with *Elden Ring* featured here having a wide assortment.

8. Advanced Soulslike Design

as a way of creating unique fights with each of the many monsters. The first major aspect you need to understand is the use of attack patterns. A "pattern" in this respect is the behavior that an enemy will do while fighting the player.

Many games that treated enemies as obstacles used a fixed pattern, meaning the enemy will perform the same thing, every time, without any deviation. You can see this in almost any 2D (two-dimensional) action/adventure or platformer released. One of the most famous examples of this is the medusa head enemy from *Castlevania* (released in 1986 by Konami). The enemy does not attack, but simply moves across the screen while bobbing up and down in a fixed sequence.

A random pattern is when an enemy's behavior will cycle between different attacks or movements. This behavior can be influenced by several factors – where the enemy is in relation to the player's character; how much health the enemy has left; or even specific conditions like if the enemy is set on fire, frozen, etc. An early example of this kind of behavior would be the original *Super Mario Bros* (released in 1985) when the player must fight Bowser at the end of each world. Bowser's behavior is built on doing specific actions: walking back and forth, shooting a fireball, jumping, and throwing hammers. The player knows all the actions that Bowser can do, but they don't know the order or what he will do next.

In early action games, it was possible to exploit the AI's (artificial intelligence) behavior – if the player knows what actions the enemy will take depending on their position, then as long as the player stays at a specific distance, they will always know what the enemy is going to do next.

The evolution that From Software brought to enemy design was to create far more advanced random patterns than anything that came before. Early games may have an enemy that has one or two attacks it can choose from; with Soulslikes, enemies can have entire sequences of attacks that they can cycle through, along with multiple conditions and types of attacks. Starting with *Dark Souls 2*, the developers saw that people were memorizing the attack patterns in their games and wanted to make it harder to fight their enemies.

A common tactic in action games is to read the enemy's attacks to know when exactly to go in and attack them. If you know that the enemy takes a long time to recover after a vertical swing of their sword, then every time you see the enemy do that attack, you immediately know it's safe to go in. What From Software started to do was give the enemy different attack patterns and have several of them start the same way, here is an example:

Pattern 1: Horizontal swing, horizontal swing, dash forward, and punch.
Pattern 2: Horizontal swing, horizontal swing, reel back their arm, vertical swing, and horizontal swing.
Pattern 3: Horizontal swing, horizontal swing, attempt to grab the character, and smash them into the ground.

Even regular enemies started to have more attack patterns and more complicated behavior. With the conditional aspect of their design, it was possible to design

Figure 8.8

A memorable boss can mean many things. From *Armored Core 6*, the Ice Worm fight is not only a visual feast, but the music and ambiance add to it, even though the player is not really "fighting" it in the same way as the other bosses in the game.

specific attack patterns the enemy could do to chase down the player, stop them from performing an attack, or unleash a stronger attack that would punish the player if they didn't get out of the way in time.

From Software began to design their enemies and bosses in two distinct ways – enemies that would attempt to mirror fighting other players, and those that completely operated differently from the player (Figure 8.8). *Demon Soul's* and *Dark Souls* both had non-playable character (**NPC**) enemies that could invade and attack the player, using similar moves and equipment as another player. Starting with *Bloodborne*, the threat level of "hunter enemies" made them some of the most challenging fights in the game, even more so in some cases compared to monsters and other demons. Often, humanoid enemies would move as fast and be able to attack as quickly and as unpredictably as fighting against other players. While monsters would have their own unique attacks, and usually, different ways of moving around, and chasing down the player.

A tactic that From Software and other soulslike designers would implement is a specific conditional attack that an enemy will do if the player's character is within a certain distance after an attack pattern is finished. For example, if the player is within a certain distance behind a character after an attack pattern, they may extend the pattern and perform a sweeping attack to try and hit the player. This attack is meant to punish aggressive players, but the problem is that it's often designed to always happen. In response, it slows down combat while the player gets in one attack, moves out of the way of the punish, and then rinse and repeat.

Most recently with *Elden Ring*, From Software wanted to force players out of their normal comfort zone for defending against attacks. Many bosses and advanced enemies would have attack patterns far longer and more damaging compared to other games. Usually, someone with a shield could just block the attacks at the loss of some stamina to then attack the enemy when they're finished. Now, the enemy is so aggressive that it's not possible to block the entire attack pattern without a large shield – the character will run out of stamina and take hits from the end of the pattern.

Before I talk about enemy balance, I want to go over the broad categories of enemies that can fit in a soulslike or action game. Unique groups of enemies can be placed in specific areas/stages of your game, but they all fall into one of the following categories:

1. Grunts – Basic enemies that do the least amount of damage, have the fewest attack patterns, and are the easiest to deal with. They are often the most numerous enemy type in an area and can prove to be a threat if they surround the player or outnumber them. There can be multiple grunt-level enemies in the same area.

2. Veterans – Tougher enemies that are a step or two above grunt-level enemies. They are more numerous than elites and supporters, but not grunts. Stronger foes that are more dangerous and can often be grouped with grunts to mix up combat encounters.

3. Supporters – Enemies designed to fill a specific role or provide a unique utility that helps other enemies in the area. This also includes range-attacking enemies who can stay back and attack the player. They are stronger than grunts, but don't show up as often. If they are alone, they can be quite easy to fight depending on their design.

4. Elites – Stronger enemies that often occupy the role of a mid-boss. They are unique enemies that are very strong to fight, have different kinds of attacks, and just one of them is usually enough to cause the player problems. Some games may introduce an elite as a boss fight before placing them normally in an area. They are strong enough that it can be very difficult to fight them if there are other enemies around.

5. Boss – An enemy that only appears one time during the game, with rare exceptions. This is a unique fight where both the enemy and the environment around them will test the player. They will always have unique attack patterns and more health than other enemies in the game and are the hardest battles for the player to win.

For every enemy type in your game, you will also need to program, balance, and animate properly all their attack patterns and motions. Part of the challenge of level design that I discussed in the last section is that it also involves enemy placement. Where you set enemies in a level, and how many at a time, greatly affects the difficulty. Fighting archers in a wide environment is easy; fighting them while trying to walk across narrow ledges as they snipe at the player is a different story. As an important point specifically about soulslike design that will come up again in Section 8.5, these games are inherently designed for the player ideally to only fight one enemy at a time. This is due to the UI of the game, and it is why you can't escalate battles as much as you can in action-focused games. In a game like *Doom Eternal*, the Doom Guy is fast and strong enough that you can throw all manner of enemies at the player at once, and they can still handle those fights. In a game like *Dark Souls*, even just two enemies at the same time can prove to be difficult. For that reason, many soulslikes will have far more diversity of enemies that can show up so that the later enemies are far more dangerous to fight even if the player is only fighting them one at a time.

Another option is to have stronger enemies who were rare in the earlier parts of the game but become more frequent in the later sections. An enemy that would be considered an elite type could be set up more frequently to fight the player. It's important to remember as a designer that the player's character can realistically focus on one enemy at a time, and to balance encounters and fights accordingly. The exception would be talking about a game that focuses on ranged attacks like *Remnant: From the Ashes*. If the player attracts, or "pulls", multiple enemies at once, it will turn into a scramble to try and thin the numbers before they are overwhelmed.

From an aesthetics standpoint, every enemy type should be visibly different from those around them. If the player is staring at a group of enemies, they need to be able to immediately spot who is the greatest threat and what each type can do. And remember how your level design is laid out will have a massive impact regarding the difficulty of fighting enemies. One of the most infamous areas in *Dark Souls 1* occurred in the first half of Anor Londo. There is a section where the player must run across narrow bridges and platforms where archers with heavy bows are aiming at them. The arrows are so strong that even if the player blocks them, the knockback was often strong enough to push them off the ledge they were on. Even if the player could reach the archer's sniping perch, they would move into melee combat with heavy shields, and the other archers could still attack the player while they were fighting (Figure 8.9).

Balancing enemy design is one of the most important aspects of any good souls-like, and if the balance is not there, it can easily ruin the experience for everyone. Part of enemy balance has to do with the pacing of your game that I'll talk about in the next section. Your enemy designs must be balanced by what the player and their character are able to do. This includes how fast the character can react, the overall strength the character can reach, their ability to dodge and block, all special moves or spells accessible, and how much health they will regularly have.

The more reactive the enemy is, the player's character must be able to respond in turn. Comparing *Elden Ring* to *Nioh*, *Elden Ring* is a far slower game with slower enemies to fight, but that goes with the speed at which the character can react. In *Nioh*, there is a major emphasis on how fast the player character is, and in response, the enemies are some of the fastest in the genre. This also means for

Figure 8.9

Enemy placement makes an enormous difference when fighting something in any reflex-driven game. This infamous section has led to many deaths in *Dark Souls 1*, and the enemy itself is not that hard to fight when the player is given room to maneuver.

soulslikes where the enemies are giving very long attack patterns; the player's character should have some way to avoid or mitigate that damage. Returning to I-frames while dodging, if the character literally can't dodge an attack pattern due to it being too fast, then that is something to investigate. Enemy speed and tells are another important point – if the enemy attacks so fast that the player can't process it, or there aren't any warnings to inform them an attack is coming, then this can lead to combat becoming frustrating and one-sided against the player. To compensate for the AI being able to react faster than the player, designers may intentionally slow down the enemy compared to the player or provide longer recovery animations that will let the player fight them a little easier. Another factor that must go into enemy balance is if the player can hit-stun or stagger the enemy. Any enemy who can be staggered either by doing enough damage or a specific move will be easier to fight than one that is stagger immune. Be aware that if you design an enemy that completely negates every form of defense and offense the player has, that can be seen as creating an imbalanced experience.

For specific enemies, it's not uncommon to see special moves that are highly damaging if the player is caught by them. From Software frequently puts in grab attacks that cannot be blocked against and will do tremendous damage if they connect. In terms of the types of attacks and attack patterns, there are no fixed rules to adhere to. Speaking of special moves, a major aspect of enemy balancing and design is the use of "tells". A tell is a specific animation or alert that the player is given for an enemy attack. The simplest example would be just the

Figure 8.10

Tells can be subtle or overt, but the player needs some way to read the enemy's actions, especially if your game is built on specific defensive maneuvers. In *Sekiro*, the kanji alert lets the player know that something very bad is about to come their way. As the game goes on, there are specific unlockable skills that can counter some of these attacks, but not grabs like the Chained Ogre is about to do.

animation itself – if the enemy reaches back with a sword, then they're obviously going to strike with it. For enemies that don't follow conventional combat or are non-humanoid, you'll need to provide the player with a way to tell when they're about to do something. In some soulslikes and action games, if the enemy is about to do something really dangerous, then the enemy will flash red or some kind of graphic or effect will appear to let the player know to get out of the way (Figure 8.10). It is important from a user experience (UX) perspective that the player is informed if an attack is coming that plays by different rules than other ones – such as something that cannot be dodged or blocked. Further still, the time between the tell and the actual attack also matters to defensive options and balancing. Some games will use a tell, and then, the attack happens immediately after. This way timing blocks or other maneuvers are synced to the tell itself. Other games may purposely use a different timing for the attack animation that will require the player to pay attention and properly time their maneuver to avoid. Here's an example of an attack that explains this further:

> Enemy rears back with a club, wait 1.5 seconds, swings club horizontally, swings club vertically, wait .75 seconds, swings club vertically.

This adds difficulty when trying to defend against attacks, but it's important to still make it something that the player can comprehend. Some games may not use any warning animations or tells – where the enemy goes from static or idle to immediately attacking, and this can be viewed as unfair to the player.

Another aspect of balancing enemy design is with how the enemy can track the player's character. Tracking can occur with both melee and ranged attacks, with the primary factors being how strong is the tracking, and how long does the enemy track for? In *Demon's Souls* and plenty of action games, enemies had very little tracking – the second the player sees the attack animation start, they can walk or dodge out of the way, and the attack will miss. The first thing that designers implemented was to increase the duration that an enemy will track the player. Here's an example:

Tracking Occurs in parenthesis (enemy bends down, enemy jumps at the player, enemy rears back for an attack) enemy starts swinging in mid-air, enemy attacks with a vertical swing.

If the player dodges at any time before the mid-air swing, the enemy will still follow the character's position and hit them. The fewer frames of animation that the player can dodge safely, the harder it will be to avoid damage. Tracking also means that the player must be more mindful as to the timing and direction of the dodge. If the player is moving left while the enemy is tracking them for an attack and dodges to the left, that attack may still connect by virtue of the enemy still swinging in the direction the player was going. Some soulslikes may introduce an item or ability that provides more I-frames during the dodge window to compensate and give players more help.

The strength of the tracking simply means how accurately will the enemy or their attack be able to follow the player. Some titles have it so strong that the enemy can start their attack facing one direction, and by the end of the attack could do a 180° spin to track the player. With ranged attacks, many soulslike designers now have a light tracking to them so that the player can't just simply take one step in either direction to avoid it. Stronger or more dangerous attacks may act like heat-seeking missiles and must either be blocked, or the character must get behind cover to avoid. For these attacks, they may also be designed to have a set duration; once it runs out, the attack will dissipate on its own.

Another aspect of frames and how they relate to soulslike design and general combat is when you are designing a 2D game. As I talked about earlier in this book, there have been attempts at translating the soulslike combat design into two dimensions. When you are designing enemies and their patterns, you must also take into consideration the number of frames of animation that attacks will show. This is not only a game design aspect, but your art and aesthetics as well. For games that tried to emulate the combat and defense-focus of the soulslikes in 3D (three-dimensional), a lot of them ran into problems when it came to the parry/riposte skills. Let's quickly go over an enemy attack's timeline in both 3D and 2D to demonstrate this:

3D: 0 second – idle, 0.25 seconds – enemy rears back for an attack, 0.50 seconds – enemy begins swinging sword, 1.00 second – enemy's sword is striking and can be parried.

In this example, the player can view all the animation frames from the enemy being idle, to preparing to swing, to swinging, to then attacking. The player can accurately tell when the enemy is in the position to be parried.

Now, here's the same attack being shown in a 2D game with fewer frames of animation:

2D: 0 seconds – idle, 0.25 seconds – enemy rears back for an attack, 1.00 second – enemy's sword is striking and can be parried.

What happened is that the game shows fewer frames of animation so that the player is only able to see the windup, and the connecting attack. This greatly increases the difficulty of parrying attacks; and in many 2D games, it's just not worth the risk if every enemy is about doing high-damage moves. To compensate, some designers will balance their combat to provide a longer window for the parry – allowing the player to stay in that stance longer so that it is easier to catch the incoming attack. Rendering more frames of animation means also creating the animations which will increase the time and money spent on your game. As an alternative, many 2D games will use a visual or audio tell for when the attack is about to happen, such as having the enemy or their weapon flash, or an ominous tone plays, so that the player doesn't need to rely on the animation frames.

The reason why this isn't a problem in 3D games is that given their design, you should not be purposely removing animation frames as that can come off as making your game look cheap. But you do need to make sure that the player can still process the attack coming at them. In action-driven games that feature non-humanoid enemies, especially ones where the enemy has no arms or a lot of arms, the animations for attacking need to be distinctive enough so that the player can recognize that there is an attack incoming (Figure 8.11).

This section has so far focused on enemy attacks and their behavior, but another defining aspect of soulslike design with their enemies is giving them defensive options. These can include the very same abilities the player has access to, or unique ones like being able to fly, teleport, etc. The enemy's ability to avoid damage is another balancing factor and will impact the difficulty of the game. As I talked about in Chapter 3 with basic action design, it's not uncommon for designers to give an enemy a means of breaking out of being stun-locked, such as automatically dodging away. The designer wants the player to be rewarded for getting in a successful hit, but they don't want to completely render the enemy useless, and this dodge is used to kind of reset the enemy's position and to let them start attacking again. For soulslikes where the player is fighting humanoid enemies, some of them may have the ability to parry the player's attack and let them perform a counterattack. The animation for being in the parry stance should be obvious to the player. As another point, be aware of how powerful the enemy's ability to defend is and avoid making it better than the player. There have been games where the enemy can literally block all damage from 360° around them, even if they are facing the opposite direction. And if the game is about the

Figure 8.11

Some of the nastiest enemies in a From Software game are the ones that aren't humanoid. *Bloodborne* on the left features a lot of monstrous bosses and enemies, and *Elden Ring* has its own assortment of animals and monsters that can be very hard to know when it's safe to go in.

enemy being able to defend against the player, the player should have some means of breaking through the defense: a heavy attack, a grab, special moves, etc.

In both *Remnant* games that focus on range attacks, several enemy types will automatically dodge the moment the player's targeting reticle is on them to make it harder for the player to quickly deal with them. If you do implement this, be aware that you don't want to make the enemy constantly perform this maneuver as it slows down the combat.

Everything I discussed in this section is all related to how you will create your combat system in your soulslike. The simplest way to define how balance works with combat is that you want the player to always have a way of dealing with an enemy. Some enemy designs will be purposely set to go against a specific player strategy – such as the enemy is programmed to be more aggressive if the player stays at a further range compared to other enemies. Many of the bosses and enemies in From Software's games are designed to have an "easy way" of fighting them – this could be using ranged attacks, parrying their attacks and going in for a counter, being aggressive, being defensive, etc. What you don't want is to have an enemy with no way of fighting them effectively. While there is the option to bring in characters or other players to team up against a boss or enemy, that should not be where you balance any encounter in a soulslike.

Be careful about designing any enemy or boss that by their design breaks the normal rules for combat or how builds work in your game. If you design a boss that negates all armor and the player can only avoid damage by properly dodging, then you are restricting options that you built into your game and punishing players for not playing in a specific fashion. Remember, there is a difference between rewarding a specific playstyle for an encounter and punishing someone for using a playstyle.

The soulslike genre is inherently a single-player experience, with coop as an option. In the *Remnant* games, they tow this line very carefully between obvious rewards and abilities designed around coop play but trying to balance and scale the encounters for single player as well. They succeed mostly, but there are still some inherent pain points to playing the series if you don't play with other players. To that last point, if you do have the ability for players to join each other's games, you will need to figure out how much the game should scale based on the number of players. In some titles, the difference between fighting a boss solo and with three people could mean almost 1.5–2 times the health bar for that fight. There should not be a boss that can only be fought in multiplayer, as that can provide an unfair disadvantage to players who are playing it solo. A unique example from *Demon's Souls* was the boss fight "Old Monk", that if the player was playing online at the time, would summon another player to fight for him. In *Dark Souls 2*, a similar situation occurred during the Mirror Knight fight who could summon other players to join it in fighting the player.

Another detail about boss designs that I haven't covered yet is with the use of phases in the fight. For especially dangerous bosses, designers may give them multiple phases that change attack patterns, behavior or completely upends the entire fight. This is one of those aspects that's entirely up to you whether to build fights around. Some people like multi-phase bosses, while others can find it tedious to die in the second or third phase and must restart the entire fight over again if they lose. The different phases may also occur all on the same health bar, such as phase 1 is at 100%–75% health, phase 2 at 74%–50%, and phase three 49%–0% (Figure 8.12).

What often distinguishes a boss fight from everything else in a game is that the arena the player is fighting them in should have an impact on the fight. You want to avoid just designing a flat area with nothing in it, but instead look at ways that the environment can interact with the boss or vice versa. Giant sand dunes could be used to block vision, or the boss could dive under the sand to attack an unsuspecting player. Often, the aesthetics of the environment can also represent the boss itself, such as fighting in their home, or something important to them. There are no requirements for what a boss "must" be in your game, but they should still be used to test the player's knowledge of how the game works.

Think of your enemy designs as an almost "combat puzzle" – there should be a challenge to it, obvious rules for how it behaves, but there needs to be a solution as well. For some bosses, they may be designed figuratively as a puzzle – where the player must use something specifically in the environment to fight them. In *Demon's Souls*, the Dragon God boss could only be defeated by reaching two ballista and use them to damage it. These can work as a kind of break between fighting strenuous enemies, but you don't want every boss in a soulslike to be a puzzle

Figure 8.12

From Software has made it a habit to design particularly challenging bosses who would be tough enough for any player to fight, but then introduce a stronger and more dangerous form for their second phase. *Elden Ring* has Malenia, Blade of Miquella as the most infamous and difficult fight in the entire game who only gets harder in her second phase.

fight, as the point of the design is to engage in combat. With that said, you are not limited to specific rules or designs for your bosses. One of the most famous boss fights in *Dark Souls* broke the rule about 1v1 combat with the Smough and Ornstein battle. The player must fight both at the same time; whoever the player kills first will lead to the remaining character becoming stronger. The more ways you can create unique encounters with your boss fights the better they will stand out and make your game memorable. Before you even begin to design an enemy and their behavior, you need to settle on how your combat system will work, and the finer points of that I'm going to talk about next.

8.3 Souls Pacing Philosophy

So far, in this chapter, I've talked about what soulslike design means for the levels, for the enemies, and now it's time to talk about the player and their character. When building and balancing a soulslike, everything that I've discussed in the previous sections stem from how you design the player's character and is another extension of the topics from Chapter 3.

To recap, what separates soulslike gameplay from other reflex-driven games is that the pacing is slower with a different focus. The number one rule of any soulslike is that rushing and not paying attention will end in disaster for the player – careful planning will always be rewarded over button mashing. Under

Figure 8.13

The power dynamics at play in a soulslike can be hard to grasp if you don't have a background studying action-based design. Enemy design must be built off what means you give the player in the form of your combat system. In *Nioh 2* here, none of the boss designs would fit in *Elden Ring* or vice versa, as both games have completely different pacing to their combat.

rare circumstances should the player ever engage with more than one enemy at a time in melee. Part of the reason ranged and spellcasting builds became popular, especially in *Elden Ring*, is that they provided the added utility of being able to hit enemies from afar, and in many cases, kill them before they can even get within range of attacking the player.

When you are designing your soulslike, you need to answer the following questions about how it's played:

1. How strong is the player's character?
2. What kind of attacks can they do?
3. What are their defensive options?
4. What are the limitations put on the player?

Again, what separates a traditional action game from a soulslike is the power disparity of the player's character with the enemies (Figure 8.13). The character is supposed to be strong, but it's not the same kind of strength seen in games like *Doom* or *Devil May Cry*. In those games, the main character walks into a room regardless of the number of enemies in it, and they are supposed to be stronger than everything in there. In a soulslike, walking into a room of enemies means that the player must slow down and figure out the best way to proceed.

The character's ability to attack is also based on the number of weapons/weapon types in the game. Obviously, there must be a generic "attack" command in your game. However, different weapons bring with them different ranges of attacks, different speeds, different damage types, and those must be factored into the design of your game.

Returning to weapon balance, let's look at two weapons we could put into a soulslike –

1. A: One-handed Spear
   - Damage Type – Thrust
   - Damage – 60
   - Attack Speed – 0.70 seconds
   - Weight – One-Handed

2. B: Giant Spear
   - Damage Type – Thrust
   - Damage – 250
   - Attack Speed – 4 seconds
   - Weight – Two-Handed

With these two weapons and no other attributes assigned to them, weapon A is by far the superior option of the two. Even though B has a far higher base damage, the amount of time it would take to swing it once, it would be possible to use A at least five times, equaling 300 damage to one swing of weapon B. To add to the problems with B, if enemies are designed to be fast, any slow-swinging weapon is automatically in trouble if the player can't dodge cancel/end the attack early. What will happen is that every time the player tries to hit the enemy, they can attack them and do damage, or possibly interrupt the attack. Often, many souls-likes struggle with balance between light, medium, and heavy-focused builds. Even if the player could compensate by wearing heavier armor and not focusing on dodging hits, if the whole point of your design is that the player should never take damage, then using these weapons would be antithetical to that approach. This was the case with the *Nioh* games and how the balance shifted into the end game and post-game content. The further the player got in the game, the more damaging enemies became, to the point where even the heaviest armor could not compensate. The final set of bosses in *Nioh* 1 all had massively damaging attacks that it was not possible to tank those hits without over-leveling for the encounter.

While that may sound cut and dry, there are ways of making this decision harder and more interesting for the player. If the player could reduce the amount of damage they take while swinging a heavier weapon, or recover health while hitting the enemy, that would provide an alternative. The "harden" ability mentioned in *Mortal Shell* was a surprisingly effective way of getting around this. As the player could start a heavy swing, if the enemy tries to hit them, harden up, let their attack get blocked, then unharden to finish the attack without taking damage. There needs to be obvious advantages and disadvantages for every weapon and every weapon type to provide the player with a variety of ways of playing. Remember this: there will always be a contingent of fans of these games who will purposely use weaker weapons and make the game harder to challenge themselves. You should never factor your balancing concerns for the hardcore minority of your fan base, as that becomes a never-ending struggle to try and keep ahead of them.

If you want to add in advance moves, keep in mind that the more actions you tie to the same button or set of inputs, the clunkier your UI will become. I'll talk more about UI/UX at the end of the chapter, but it's important when designing the different attacks and moves a character can do to not overwhelm the player. Earlier in this book, I stated that soulslikes removed a lot of the complexity of playing a traditional action game, along with adding in RPG progression. Some games have tried to add that complexity back in by giving characters more moves they can perform and more to keep track of while playing. Part of getting the combat right in this genre is focusing on quality over quantity, and that also has to do with the number of attack options. And to that point, if the player figures out that one attack is the best out of everything available, they will just keep using that and ignore everything else available. *Nioh* had an interesting way of getting around this with the different stances. The higher the stance, the stronger the character's attack, but it would slow down their dodge. Advanced play often had players dodging in low stance where it was easier to get behind an enemy to then switch to high stance for the most damage.

When I talked about enemy design and balance, I mentioned the use of recovery frames, or the frames in which a character is returning to a neutral position and before they can respond again. Recovery frames are also a factor for the player's character and can have a huge impact on the difficulty and pacing of your combat system. The more frames that the player's character is unresponsive, the harder it will be to react to enemy attacks. This can literally be a difference in milliseconds in terms of making your combat easier or harder. Here's a quick example of how if the recovery frames are too long, it can lead to combat not feeling right:

Player: 00:00 – player hits attack button, 00:25 – character starts swing, 00:50 – character strikes, 00:50 to 01:25 – recovery frames.

In this example, the player must wait 0.75 seconds after an attack before they are able to respond to anything else. While that doesn't sound long, if an enemy attacks like this:

Enemy: 00:00 – enemy starts attack animation, 00:35 – enemy strikes, 00:35 to 00:45 – recovery frames.

If the enemy starts their attack while the player has just hit the attack button, it will start, and hit the character before the player's character can finish their

Figure 8.14

It is hard to make it out due to the speed, but dodging on the left in a From Software soulslike always grants I-frames and can be used to avoid most attacks. Parrying on the right only works against specific enemies and specific attacks, but, if mastered, can completely shut down some opponents.

animation. Without any means of animation canceling, it means the player is committed to every swing no matter what. This becomes even more important if we're talking about soulslikes that are defensive-focused and that the player needs to be always ready to block, dodge, or parry an enemy attack. Like I said further up, the differences between something feeling right or wrong can come down to milliseconds.

Defense is a key aspect of soulslike and action design and is another point that can ruin your game if not handled properly. As I discussed in Chapter 3, defensive options are there to mitigate or remove the damage of an incoming attack – the easier the option to do, the least effective it should be. You should try to have at least two ways of avoiding damage in your game – one that is more general/easier to do and one that rewards proper timing (Figure 8.14). Sometimes, these options can be one and the same. Many action games will give the player a "dodge", and dodging at any time is the safe way of avoiding damage. However, if the player times the dodge to the moment just before an attack hits, they may be rewarded with the chance of doing more damage. One of the first examples of this was *Bayonetta* (released in 2009 Platinum Games), and performing a perfect dodge granted the player "witch time" that slowed all the enemies down and opened them up to increased damage. And remember, the more I-frames that you build into the dodging animation, the easier it will be to perform. Also, having I-frames is not required; there are games where dodging simply gets the player's hitbox away from the attack but does not grant them any I-frames. While this is an option, it will make your game a lot harder and something to note when balancing.

With the act of parrying, how you time it is going to greatly impact the difficulty and its utility in the game. In the *Dark Souls* series, parrying itself does not happen the instant the player hits the button. When the character is performing the animation, there is a set window during the swing of the shield or parrying dagger where they will parry. If they do it too soon, then the enemy will hit before the animation plays out; too late, and the character will get caught at the start of the animation. Like with dodging, the more frames where the character can parry, the easier it will be to perform. Some games have what's called a "perfect parry"; that if the player times the parry so that it connects at the "sweet spot" of the animation, said sweet spot is different per game, it will have a greater impact or set up the enemy to take more damage. In games where parrying is the focus, designers may make the parry instantaneous – the second the player hits the button, the character's animation is parrying. This is for games where combat is very fast, and often, the player may have to parry multiple hits in the span of seconds to fully stop the attack, such as with *Sekiro*.

As blocking is the most basic defensive move, there isn't really a lot to say about it. Usually, the only consideration that goes with it is whether the player is using a piece of equipment that can block. The *Dark Souls* trilogy and *Elden Ring* do allow the player to use weapons to block, allowing someone to have a more aggressive combat style instead of just relying on blocking. The downside is that no matter what weapon the player uses, it will never be as good at blocking, or mitigating as much damage compared to a shield. As a form of balancing, From Software implemented different degrees of absorbing damage into their shields to further differentiate them from each other. A weaker shield may only block 75% of incoming damage, while something far heavier and harder to use could block 95%–100% of incoming damage. If your game has different kinds of damage, shields and blocking can be set to block differing amounts of each type. If your game has stamina, then you will also need to consider how much stamina is used on a per-shield basis. The stronger the shield often means that it will use up less stamina per individual hit compared to a lighter shield.

When building your defensive options, you want to make sure that enemy attacks are transparent as to what options will work on them. Typically, in From Software's design, the player can parry, block, or dodge any attack from humanoid enemies or those that are around the same size as them. When they are fighting larger enemies, or those with over-the-top attacks, it may not be possible to parry them. Whereas with other franchises, they may allow the player to parry literally any attack in the game no matter what.

One detail to be mindful of is how required advanced defensive moves are to being able to play your game, as that will have an impact on the difficulty. In many of From Software's games, the parry can greatly reduce the difficulty of fighting some bosses and harder enemies, but it's not required to stand a chance against them. In both *The Surge* games, blocking doesn't stop damage but simply reduces the incoming amount. To completely avoid damage, players had to time ducks and hops by holding blocks and pressing down and up to avoid high and low attacks, respectively. The problem with this system was there was no secondary association or graphical user interface (GUI) element to inform the player what kind of attack the next hit was, and guessing wrong was very punishing in the game. To help mitigate this, one of the passive options unlocked in the sequel was to add a GUI element that informs the player as to what correct dodge to use on the next attack. If you are targeting your game to a hardcore market, such as with *Sifu*, then this system can work, but it will create an even higher skill floor for people to be able to play your game.

The challenge of creating defensive options is that you want to avoid having one that is too good – if the player can use a tactic that stops all damage, that's easy to do, and there's no penalty for failure, then the combat system can feel flawed to the player. However, if you introduce an enemy who has no defensive option that works against them, then the player will feel like the game is cheating them. And from an onboarding perspective, you need to educate the player on how defensive options and their advanced strategies will work. As an example of what not to do, in *Wo Long: Fallen Dynasty*, the game was set up around parrying enemy blows as the main defensive move, with blocking as your fallback strategy. However, unlike every soulslike that came before it, the player could parry while blocking – completely making the act of parrying safe to do. The problem is that none of that was conveyed in the tutorial text, if it wasn't for a fan pointing it out while I was playing, I would have never known that, because soulslikes are not typically designed that way.

The one point that ties this section together and differentiates soulslikes from everything else is the limiting factors against the player. To slow down the player, and by extension the combat, there needs to be a limitation that prevents them from button mashing and focusing only on being aggressive. The most common example of this, as I mentioned earlier in the book, is having a stamina resource. The character can only attack provided they have enough stamina; run out, and they will become unable to defend or attack until the meter fills up again. Stamina usage and recovery can further be balanced based on the character's equipment load, passive upgrades, and other factors.

You want there to be a risk of heavy aggression by the player and the threat of running out of stamina at the worst moment. A newer feature soulslikes are doing starting with *Elden Ring* is removing the stamina drain for running and basic options when the player is not in combat. This allows someone to explore as fast as they can and reduces the need to constantly keep waiting for stamina to regenerate to run again.

And one last point before I move on, the defensive options I've discussed in this section are not set in stone for action or soulslike design. Just like with RPG systems that I discussed in *Game Design Deep Dive: Role Playing Games*, you are free to decide what options will form the basis of your gameplay, and then, you need to figure out how to balance them in your game. Returning to *Bloodborne*, the game was purposely designed to remove blocking as a core defensive option, and in turn, dodging and parrying were made stronger. More options will make things easier, as people can gravitate toward the one they are most comfortable with, but they still need to be balanced within the confines of your design.

One aspect that isn't really touched on when it comes to soulslikes is player vs. player or PVP content. While these games have been focused on the single player, or player vs. the environment (PVE) content, there has been some interest in having PVP areas in them. From Software games often have a guild or side quest that involves going out there and invading other player's games and collecting a resource used to further the quest. There is also the option of having dedicated "PVP zones" where players can meet and fight each other. PVP is something that needs to be optional for these games, as they are often hard enough without needing other players adding to the difficulty. The attraction of PVP is aligned with the nature of customization presented in these games. Often, PVP players can create very unusual builds and strategies that wouldn't work against an AI opponent but can be something surprising against a human one. However, if you decide to go the route of PVP, you need to be aware of how there is a difference between PVE and PVP balance. This is a challenge that is never-ending and is why many designers will create specific balancing for PVE and PVP separately. You do not want to make the PVE side of your game harder because gamers found a very powerful PVP strategy. An easy way to avoid this conflict is to have specific rules in place for how skills behave when used against another player vs. an NPC.

Good pacing and progression in a soulslike is about the player becoming better at the game alongside their character. There needs to be a sense of mastery to your gameplay – something to reward the players who truly learn how your game works. Many of From Software's games over the 2010s had final bosses that felt easier to fight than the enemies that came before them. This wasn't due to them being designed easier, but that the players who could reach them were masters at the game, and these bosses served as one final test of their abilities. You don't want your game to feel like the player has seen and learned everything within one hour of playing – there needs to be something new – a new weapon to try, a new environment to explore, new enemies, etc. (Figure 8.15). Even if you are designing your game to be on the easier side to learn, there must still be progression built into the pacing of your game if you want to motivate people to keep playing. If the moment-to-moment gameplay of your soulslike feels boring or repetitive after a while, then you are not designing your game right. This can also extend to weapon design and the different builds. Earlier in this book, I mentioned how people would try to play these games under specific limitations or rules. There are also people who want to figure out a build that just demolishes everything in your game and try to put that into action.

The first three sections in this chapter should demonstrate to you the differences in how you need to approach building a soulslike from a level, enemy, and player character standpoint. These three aspects need to stand out, and why it's a hard genre to work in as a new designer. It's very easy to focus on only one of

Figure 8.15

Mortal Shell condensed the soulslike experience down into four areas including the hub to explore. But it severely lacked the variety of challenges and enemies that are typically seen in the genre. And the level and environmental design within each area was not unique enough to keep players from getting lost or turned around.

them, and why many people view the ones by From Software in such high regard. At the end of the day, the goal of these games is to create a very specific experience for the player – challenging them to learn how the game works, explore a variety of levels, and defeat a variety of enemies. Again, I need to point out that this is not an easy subgenre to make a game in, and why From Software has yet to be dethroned by any other studio with their takes.

To end this section, I have one final point that you should take to heart when building your combat system and enemies in your game. The player needs to feel like they are fighting the enemies in your game and not the mechanics or camera. Returning to difficulty, it's easy to look at something hard and think that it's good or balanced, but if something is difficult because the game doesn't work right, then you are going to end up with a poor soulslike. I feel there are designers who look at any of From Software's games and think "I can make that better," but the details of how combat feels in the player's hands are what will determine whether your game will succeed. Getting that feel right takes a lot of time analyzing combat systems and making sure that yours will work for people other than yourself and your friends. There's a difference between an enemy that is challenging because it is well designed and one that is frustrating because the animations and camera prevent the player from seeing incoming attacks. You cannot rely on being "new" for people to give it a pass on issues, as they can always go back and play any of From Software's hits.

8.4 Lore vs. Plot in Soulslikes

Storytelling is not a focus of this Deep Dive, but it's important to at least explain some of the common aspects that soulslikes use. Returning to *Demon's Souls* and then all throughout From Software's games, they set a very specific trend of how their games work from a narrative point of view.

When we talk about storytelling in video games, especially for narrative-driven ones, there are two specific areas of building the story – the lore and the plot of a game. To make things easy, we can define the two as the following:

> Lore – the story of the world itself
> Plot – the story of the main character(s)

Many games that feature different or unusual settings will build the lore into the world itself; this is where the term "environmental storytelling" originates (Figure 8.16). A popular use of this is in the "dystopian" setting, where the world around the player is already destroyed, and they can put the pieces together by looking at the remains. In this respect, the player, and by extension their character, has no impact on the lore; this is something that has long since happened

Figure 8.16

Environmental storytelling has been around since the early days of the game industry, but it really took off in the nineties and through to the 2000s as developers started to get more creative with their worlds. One of the most famous examples is the *Bioshock* series by Irrational Games. The first two took place in an undersea dystopic world inspired by Ayn Rand where players saw the aftermath of the collapse. In the third game picture here, it took place in the flying city Columbia, where players got to witness the city at its peak before things came down.

8. Advanced Soulslike Design

to the world of the game. The horror genre has also made extensive use of this form of storytelling. Instead of the player/character trying to impact the world, it's more about their experience in this setting, and often, trying to escape it in the case of horror games.

Lore is popular because it adds more weight to the experience and gives the player a deeper sense of meaning to what is going on. There are games that people have made multi-hour-long videos trying to break down and explain the lore of the setting. Lore can also be grown from game to game and can become a kind of Easter egg for fans who have been following a franchise. However, focusing only on lore and nothing else when coming up with the narrative can leave the game feeling hollow. This is part of the problem that indie horror games have struggled with by focusing exclusively on lore. There is no investment in the current state of things or the main character; the main character is not driving any form of storytelling or the narrative. Another form of this is the "silent protagonist" or when the player controls someone who has no emotion, no stakes, and no impact on the world or story around them. The silent protagonist is often used as a means of having a story where there is a main character, but that character is simply a cipher in which the player is the one who gets to experience things. A variation of this is where the player chooses an archetype who may come with a base personality and a collection of catchphrases and barks, but the story was built so that any character can be copied and pasted into it without missing a beat. The massively multiplayer online game (**MMOG**) genre was one of the biggest examples of this kind of storytelling as their whole attraction was building a world that could fit thousands of players and letting them explore and discover things. A counter to this would be in the recent *Doom* games; while the Doom Guy doesn't talk, the game still shows his mannerisms that express what he's thinking and feeling.

Some games try to have it both ways, and let the player decide a base personality for their character, or the character may talk or offer some generic input during cutscenes. But this can still leave the narrative feeling plain when the character can only say stock answers or emotions instead of having a fully realized main character. Another option is to let the player have full control over how the character plays and their abilities, but they are controlling a named character with their own agency and narrative. A good example of this would be *The Witcher* series by CD Projekt Red (first released in 2007), where the player is always controlling the series' star: Geralt of Riva and can decide how he grows and what decisions he will make, but they are all still filtered through his personality.

Conversely, the plot represents the story that is happening to the main character, or the character the player creates at the start of the game. This is their specific impact on the world and needs to answer the following questions:

- What is the main character doing?
- What are the stakes?
- How do they feel about what's going on?

...This is your fate.

Figure 8.17

The *Dark Souls* series does have a plot as to what the player's goal is and the stakes of the situation, but none of that is mentioned or reflected in the character. We are never given a chance to see what our character thinks of things or even responding to bosses and NPCs monologuing.

With soulslikes, the player is not controlling a specific person in the world, and this is by design (Figure 8.17). In the From Software games, they are supposed to be playing as someone who is considered unimportant by everyone around them – a lower-class dreg who must rise from their situation and position to change the world around them. This is also the reason why the normal ending in From Software's soulslikes has the player's character becoming a king or ruler and changing the trajectory of the world going forward. But here's the dirty little secret: these games are often very poor when it comes to storytelling and plot because of their focus on lore. Boss enemies and NPCs will talk to the player's character, but that character has no response or any emotion about the world around them. One could argue that the character is simply meant to be the extension of the player.

This is a tough point for designers to tread because narrative is often considered an afterthought in reflex-driven games. For many action games, the story could be summed up by this:

- You're a good guy.
- There's a bad guy doing something bad.
- Go stop them.

Anything that stops or interrupts the player from focusing on the core gameplay loop, or in this case – exploring and fighting, is usually considered a negative.

Figure 8.18

Hades is the rare example of a game that ties the roguelite progression to the very nature of the story and dialogue of the characters while telling an engaging story in-between the runs.

From Software also popularized another form of integrating lore into the narrative with their items. As I mentioned earlier in the book, every single piece of equipment, weapon, consumable, and general item that the player can collect has a story to it and how it relates to the world. This was their solution to get around creating a very in-depth world, but not forcing the player to investigate it if they don't want to. Part of those multi-hour videos I mentioned are people literally examining every single lore description in the game to try and understand the world of the game.

Here's the question that I'm sure you are wondering: Which one is better to focus on? There is no easy answer to this, especially for soulslikes. For games where the narrative is the focal point, then, obviously, you need a strong plot to motivate someone to keep playing and see where it goes. In a reflex-driven game, you want to keep the player engaged with the gameplay, and that's when having a light plot and a lore-heavy focus can help. As of writing this book in 2023, there hasn't been a soulslike yet where the player is controlling a unique character with their own agency and impact on the plot at the time of writing this book.

Personally, I view lore and plot in games as the icing on the cake – they will not make a bad game good, but they can elevate a great game further. Part of the growth of game design in the 2010s was a greater appreciation for storytelling and tying that to a great gameplay loop. *Hades* by Supergiant Games (officially released in 2019) managed to weave the story they wanted to tell through the conventions and design of a roguelite, leading to a game that was greater than the sum of its parts (Figure 8.18).

8.5 Soulslike UI/UX Design

UI/UX work is an essential part of any game's design and especially true for genres that are known to be hard to play. Every genre has its own specific rules and conventions that you need to understand when building your game. Because soulslikes feature both action and RPG design, it means you are going to have to make sure that both aspects are given equal treatment from a UI/UX perspective (Figure 8.19).

Continuing the discussion from Chapter 3, the first thing you should be thinking of is how the UI of your game is going to work. This means figuring out the number of commands that will be in your game and how you will set that up on a gamepad and keyboard and mouse interface. From Software's UI has become the accepted standard for soulslikes, and while it has changed slightly over the years, and I'll point out some of the differences in later games further down, this is a good start if you are new to designing a soulslike.

	PlayStation	Xbox	Keyboard+ Mouse
Move	Left Stick	Left Stick	WSAD
Adjust Camera	Right Stick	Right Stick	Mouse
Interact	X	A	Q
Dodge	O	B	Space
Run	Hold Dodge	-	-
Use Item	Square	X	E
Two-hand Mode	Triangle	Y	Left Alt
Normal Attack	R1	Right Button	Left Click
Heavy Attack	R2	Right Trigger	Shift+ Normal
Block	L1	Left Button	Left Shift
Parry	L2	Left Trigger	Tab

This list represents the basic commands that have been relatively unchanged in terms of being featured in soulslikes. A few things to note: when you are building your combat system and quality of life (QOL) features, adding or removing any of these elements will result in you changing button assignments. I did not include advanced commands and shortcuts, as those will be dependent on how you design your game. Typically, the fewer buttons that are required to play the game, the more streamlined your UI is going to be.

While this is a great place to get started, don't assume that this arrangement is set in stone. Series like *Nioh* featured a radically different UI as there was the added element of allowing the player to change their stance during combat and activate ki pulses to recover their ki. Also, with *Nioh*, it used a form of UI design that I like to call a "modifier button." Modifier buttons are held down to change the behavior of other buttons. By holding down R1 (or RB on a Xbox gamepad), this modified the left, top, and bottom buttons to let the player change the stance

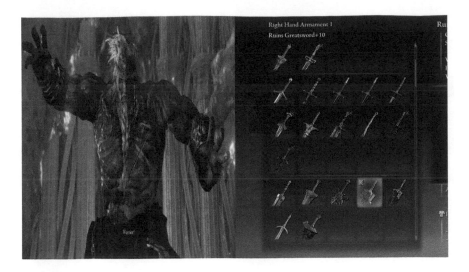

Figure 8.19

Creating an attractive and functional UI and GUI may not be as exciting as designing an epic boss fight, but these games, more so than other genres due to their high skill curve, live or die based on how they feel to play in the player's hands.

of their character. When From Software released *Elden Ring*, one of the major changes they made to the UI was assigning "jump" to what was considered "interact" previously. This was done for several reasons. The A button (or X on a PlayStation controller) is most used as the jump button in platformers, and with jumping becoming a primary action in *Elden Ring*, it was necessary to assign it a button that everyone would immediately recognize and could easily hit while playing. And remember, whatever actions are considered primary by your core gameplay loop, those need to be set to their own buttons on the UI.

This section is also a good time to bring back the use of affordances mentioned in Section 3.2. If you look at the normal attack and block commands above, characters in the game will wield a weapon in their right hand and a shield or secondary piece of equipment in their left. By assigning the attack commands to the right button and trigger, it creates an affordance and secondary association to the player – knowing that the right part of the controller is for attacking, and the left part is for defense. To go back to *Nioh* modifier example, by making the left, top, and bottom face buttons change the character's stance to normal, high, and low, respectively, it provides another association of the button's placement to the type of stance. While this may sound simple to you reading this, it is very easy to make your UI unnecessarily frustrating to learn if you ignore the layout of the controller, and the player's hand placements when assigning commands. And to that point, if you are thinking about how to set up shortcuts for advanced commands, besides using the left analog stick, it is only possible for a player to comfortably press one of the back left buttons, one of the back right buttons,

Figure 8.20

This screenshot encompasses all the GUI elements that you can see at one time during combat in *Elden Ring*. Notice how most of the GUI elements are on the corners, keeping the center of the screen clean. And the game will hide most of these elements when the player is not fighting any enemies.

and two face buttons that are close to each other. Any more than that and it can become uncomfortable at minimum and just plain confusing to do at worst on the player's part.

With the keyboard and mouse, it is by far the hardest interface to play a souslike, as it's not set up to provide the same kind of affordances and hand positioning that a gamepad does. If you are releasing your game on the PC, you still need to assume that someone may play it with a keyboard and mouse, or you can say on your store page that keyboard and mouse are not supported and just ignore it.

Moving to the graphical user interface (GUI), the main screen for action games is kept as clean as possible, as you want the player to focus on the character and what's happening around them (Figure 8.20). A popular style is to use the corners and edges of the screen to display important information. This can also create a soft framing effect, where information is set up around the actual main screen. You still need to make those GUI elements stand out enough so that the player can quickly view them in the heat of combat. To that point, the most important information – health and the character's stamina – will be positioned so that the player does not need to adjust their viewing angle that much to view it while still focusing on the character. In From Software's games where the main character is kept roughly in the middle of the screen, health and stamina are displayed in the top-left corner. In a game like *Remnant*, where the character is kept at the bottom of the screen while aiming occurs directly in the middle, this information is moved to the bottom of the screen.

Both soulslikes and action games may use color or symbols to indicate specific threats against the player. This could be anything from a warning when the enemy is going to perform a powerful attack, to using color to indicate what kind of element the enemy is, and many more. Using color and symbols can clash with the aesthetics of your game, or overwhelm the player's viewpoint, and need to be used on a case-by-case basis. If there is a focus on different elements or types of damage having a huge factor in how combat plays out, then there needs to be a way to demonstrate that to the player. You can use aspects like different hit effects or different colored numbers to inform the player if something is weak or resistant to their attack.

Before I move on to talking about the RPG UI, I want to touch on QOL elements that can be set up on the action side. One of the most important to include is a lock-on system. By pressing the button, which soulslikes often default to L3 (pushing the left analog stick in), the game will automatically target the closest enemy and take over camera manipulation while the lock-on is in effect. This is very important to help the player focus on fighting and to reduce the complexity of the controls during that time. It should also be possible to keep the lock-on up, but switch targets if need be. For ranged weapons, a lock-on is necessary to let someone use those attacks while in the process of fighting and dodging an enemy. In third- and first-person shooters, they can also employ what is known as a soft lock-on – once the player puts the targeting reticle on an enemy, the game will try and keep it on the enemy without needing further aiming. This is often used when someone is playing a shooter using a gamepad instead of a keyboard and mouse. Many competitive games will disable this or reduce its effectiveness to keep someone from having an unfair advantage. Depending on the design of the melee weapons and the camera system itself, you may need to have a lock-on system for the player to actually hit anything.

Speaking of the camera, due to the melee focus of most soulslikes (*Remnant* notwithstanding), you want to make sure that the camera remains mostly fixed to keep the player character around the middle of the screen. This is because the player needs to be able to see all around the character and where they are in relation to hazards and enemies around them. They should still be able to adjust the pitch and rotation if need be, and there should be a command to reset the camera back to its default view. Many action games will sometimes completely change the view of the camera to make things more cinematic or force the player to focus on something, this is not allowed in a soulslike – the player must always be given the best possible viewpoint for fighting and exploring.

Another hard element of your camera is what to do when characters are either too close to each other or the player's character is up against a wall. For a lot of soulslikes and action games, the in-game camera can get stuck on walls or objects and get pushed into the character model, making it nearly impossible to see the enemy or any obstacles. One way around this is to build into the programming that if the camera gets pushed into a wall, it will make the wall transparent to allow it to keep viewing the player at the optimal angle. For large enemies – those that are four times larger or even more than the player – camera systems that

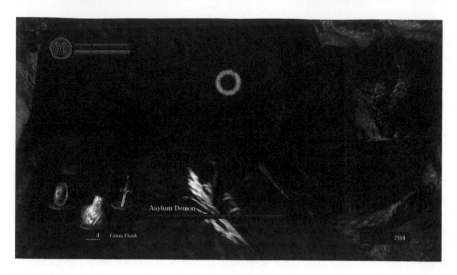

Figure 8.21

No matter what soulslike we are talking about, they all suffer from the camera having trouble with fighting large enemies. This sight here is quite common, and there's no easy solution without completely changing the camera system.

keep the player in a specific part of the screen suffer during these fights, even if the player uses a lock-on (Figure 8.21). Typically, the lock-on will keep the player character at a specific distance away from the targeted enemy, allowing it to only worry about rotation. With large enemies, however, because it takes up more of the screen, the camera can't keep the whole enemy in frame. This can lead to situations where it only shows the legs or the chest of the enemy, and the player can't see incoming attacks or even their own character model. Even if the camera does stay far enough away, when the character goes in close to fight it, the camera can get stuck on the enemy's model and leads to the player having to fight without any vision of their character. Some action games get around this by zooming out during large fights or displaying them from a specific angle. Unfortunately, this solution doesn't work for soulslikes since they always keep focus on the player's character. There is no easy solution for this, and even From Software has yet to find the perfect camera system for their games. In my opinion, viewability is king, and I would prefer having a specific camera position that provides the best view of the fight, even if that means changing the viewpoint for those battles.

On the RPG side, some of this I already covered in *Game Design Deep Dive: Role Playing Games*, but I will focus on what's relevant here. This is where you are going to focus on making the abstract elements of the game as clear as possible. You are going to need screens for displaying the character's attributes, all items and equipment, and making sure that this makes as much sense to the player. A simple, but effective GUI element is with the use of dynamic tooltips and information. Dynamic refers to GUI elements that update in real-time based on what the player is doing and looking at. An example of this is when someone is comparing two different pieces of gear, the game will show the differences between wearing gear A vs. gear B, allowing someone to easily spot what will change if they swap gear around. If the player can't use a specific piece of gear for any reason, the game should convey why to the player. You also want to include ways of sorting the player's backpack of items. Soulslikes are notorious for having lots of different equipment pieces, key items, consumable items, notes, etc. If someone wants to find a specific type of item, there should be a way to sort and filter the screen to show the relevant information easily.

A useful feature for any game that has a focus on exploration is having a map screen. The map will either update in real-time based on where the player is exploring, or the player could buy a map from a vendor that will then update the main one. Map functionality is a debated feature; some like the idea of being able to view everything around them and chart a course to the next required area. Others like the feeling of just getting lost in the world and navigating through using the environment itself. If you are trying to make your game approachable, then having a map screen is an important feature to keep people from getting lost. In the older soulslikes where each area was self-contained, a map wasn't as necessary, but as the size of these games grew, and with *Elden Ring* being an open world, the player needs a way to see where they are at any given time. You should also allow players to place markers on the map to let them remember where things were located, but the game should automatically do that for details like fast travel points, quest locations and quest givers, essential resources, important events, or anything that the player needs to interact with over the course of playing.

A debated point of some soulslikes is being able to pause the game. While this doesn't sound like a big deal, for those that have multiplayer options, it isn't possible for one player to stop everything while there are other people in the same game. As a UX feature, being able to stop things and step away is something that is important to people. A part of the challenge and planning that goes into playing these games is setting up important items and skills for the various hotkeys before the player goes into battle. This is often the defense that people give against being able to pause the game. I always find challenging the player to speed through menus to be frustrating. I'm of the opinion that it should be possible at minimum to pause the game if it's being played in single-player mode.

In earlier chapters, I brought up the use of fast travel, and for the soulslike market today, this is a non-negotiable point. As the size of these games grew, so have the amount of walking and backtracking required to visit a new area. This can be compounded by the fact that the player is visiting areas where the enemies are now so weak to them that it's not even worth it to fight them anymore. Fast travel allows someone to get back to a previously visited area instantly and is essential today if you expect anyone to try and explore everything in a game. In *Elden Ring*, many side quests could require exploring all over the massive continents. There are light, medium, and heavy versions of fast travel that designers will employ based on their games. The light version is about specific "fast travel

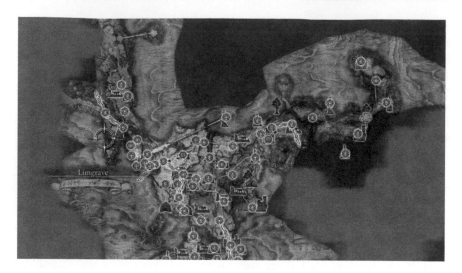

Figure 8.22

Fast travel has gone from being "nice to have," to an unlockable, to now something people expect from the very beginning of the game. *Elden Ring* tied its fast travel to the added map, but other soulslike may just have a selectable list of locations depending on the size of the game.

stations" set up throughout the world that the player can warp from one to the other. The next step up is that specific checkpoints/bonfires act as fast travel, still requiring the player to return to one to travel. Lastly, every checkpoint/bonfire is a fast travel station, and the player can teleport to them instantly provided they are not in direct combat. Some games allows the player to fast travel but only by using a consumable item. While this can add difficulty to the game, it is not a popular option in games that are already on the harder side as is. When we talk about providing a qualitative experience, reducing the amount of time backtracking is an essential aspect of this (Figure 8.22).

One last detail about the GUI of your game, and this should be obvious, but I need to make sure that everyone reading this knows it. Every game regardless of its genre needs a functional "options" menu to let them do everything from video, audio, performance, and gameplay-effecting elements, including rebinding controls.

Soulslikes by their very design are often harder to get into compared to other genres, and why proper UI/UX design is important to consider. This will not only help you when it comes to designing them, but also improve your own sense of design. I always say when it comes to UI/UX, while it's not the glamorous side of game development, it is one of the easiest ways to sink your game if done incorrectly. A good way to study UI/UX is to play other games in the genre and look at conventions that you liked or disliked about playing them. And remember, just because a popular game gets away with having issues with their UI/UX, it does not mean you are allowed to do the same.

The Future of Soulslikes

9.1 How *Elden Ring* Redefined the Genre

Throughout this book, I've referenced *Elden Ring* in passing, and it's finally time to look closer at the game. This is the one that prompted me to write this Deep Dive on soulslikes, and it is without a doubt the most successful game From Software has put out since its inception to date. And with it, they have easily set a new benchmark for soulslikes for the rest of this decade (Figure 9.1).

From the outside, it may be easy to think that *Elden Ring* was just a soulslike but bigger, but a lot was done to make it different from previous games. This is the first soulslike to go fully open world. The closest a soulslike came to an open-world structure was *Ashen*, but it did not have the same scope and scale. In the last chapter on level and environmental design, soulslikes featured transitionary areas that were meant to connect major stages to one another and flesh out the scope of the world. This created the sense of being an open world while still having a linear path through it, but *Elden Ring* is the real thing; it is by far the largest game space From Software has made in a soulslike.

In this respect, *Elden Ring* borrows more from the structure of open-world RPGs as opposed to other soulslikes. While this does dilute some of the control

DOI: 10.1201/9781003450078-9

Figure 9.1

Elden Ring's success marks the highest point that soulslikes have reached to date, and it is unclear if we will see another studio this decade attempt their own take on an open-world soulslike.

and pacing of previous games, those elements are still there in the form of the points of interest. Being open world gives players of soulslike games for the first time the freedom to go anywhere they want. After the tutorial, the player awakens on a continent near the southern point of the world. From there, they can explore this area as long as they want, head east to other areas, or focus on going north to the main path of the story. The points of interest in *Elden Ring* are designed to incentivize exploring the world and provide the player with the means of improving their build.

The points of interest are categorized into different types:

- Tombs – Mini dungeons where the player can find the resources for upgrading and acquiring new summons.
- Mines – Dungeons where the player can get the upgrade material for their weapons.
- Gravesites – one room challenges that either have a boss or minions with a treasure at the end.
- Towers – a puzzle that awards the player with the ability to equip more spells at once.
- Events – Situations that occur out in the field with each one different.
- Evergaols – arenas where the player can fight a boss for rewards.
- Quest Givers – People with quests for the player to try and complete.
- Forts – Smaller castles with minions to fight and treasure at the end.

- Hero's Graves – Larger tombs with treasure to find, punctuated by having to dodge massive chariots that roam the halls.
- Vendors – Characters that sell different items.
- Legacy Dungeons – The actual major stages complete with their unique boss for the player to fight.

While this list may sound large, these are all spread out across the massive game space – giving each one room to breathe in the world itself, while being completely optional with the exception to some of the legacy dungeons. The official "main path" through the *Elden Ring* requires the player to go north from the starting location and reach Leyndell, and there are two routes to reach the part of the continent where it's located. However, to complete the area and move on to what is considered the back half of the game, the player must have collected at least two great runes, these are only found by beating the major bosses in the game and they are in specific areas (Figure 9.2).

The ability to go anywhere that the player wants within reason gives the game a far different sense of pacing compared to previous titles. The different points of interest that have upgraded materials will let the player become stronger and give them a better chance when it comes time to attempt the major areas. There are more ways of building a character in *Elden Ring* compared to previous entries. The biggest change is with the option to find summons that let the player bring their own NPC helper into a fight. These NPCs come in different varieties, have different utilities, and can be upgraded to provide more help. In return, it allows

Figure 9.2

The first two Elden Lords players will run into could not be further apart in terms of fighting them. As a bonus, each Elden lord will provide the player with a great rune, with each one having a unique benefit for equipping it.

someone who is playing the game by themselves to still have backup during fights.

Speaking of fighting, *Elden Ring* has some of the most advanced and hardest enemy patterns in a soulslike, and it's difficult to say whether it or the *Nioh* series is the hardest overall. The reason is due to bosses and enemies having more "wild combos" – where they will perform 4 or more attacks in a single attack string. For close-ranged characters, you literally cannot block the entire combo unless you heavily invested in a grand shield. For dodging, the timing of the dodge to avoid all the attacks is very precise. This comes to a head with the game's optional boss – Malenia, who not only has very hard attacks to avoid, but she regains health whenever she hits the player. Even though *Nioh* is played at a faster speed, the player's character is also highly responsive to compensate for the patterns. In *Elden Ring*, the player character's response time and animation speed are still on the slower side.

Of the different ways of playing *Elden Ring*: melee, ranged, spellcasting, summoning, the developers have balanced boss fights and encounters on the player using at least two or more of these strategies. If someone goes in pure melee, then groups of enemies and the more dangerous bosses can wear the player down. All magic or range means that aggressive enemies who can stay close will destroy the player. That hasn't stopped the hardcore fans from declaring certain strategies as the "correct way to play."

Changing to an open-world design also changed how movement and exploration worked. In the last chapter regarding UI/UX, I mentioned having a map and fast travel options, which *Elden Ring* has both from the start. Due to the amount of ground covered, one of the early unlocks is to get a spirit horse named Torrent, who can be summoned at any time in outside areas (they will not appear in enclosed areas and legacy dungeons). Riding Torrent not only lets the player move faster, but they are able to fight on horseback. The downside is that if Torrent gets hit too many times, it will disappear, and the player will be left vulnerable.

Being able to jump as a primary action also changed the level design, with leaping onto platforms now a requirement for progress. Players could also perform a new jumping attack that did more stagger damage to enemies, with jumping also required to avoid specific ground attacks.

With all that said, the open-world structure does leave *Elden Ring* with one weakness. The game has a bit of a problem when it comes to early onboarding, both in terms of the new structure, and the general challenge of soulslikes. In fact, many people misconstrued the tutorial as just another trap the designers laid out and avoided it in their first play (Figure 9.3). When someone leaves the tutorial section, they are told that they can follow golden wisps of light to guide them. Doing so will take the player to Stormveil Castle – the first legacy dungeon where they can find a great rune. The problem is that for someone new, heading straight for the castle with no preparation or skill at the game is going to end badly for them when they run into Margit the Fell Omen. In return, fans of open-world games did the opposite and explored the rest of the continent before

Figure 9.3

Sometimes, building a reputation that your games are meant to be hard can come back to haunt you. Many players thought that the tutorial: the cave of knowledge, was just another trap for unsuspecting players. The game was updated with this message to let people know that without a doubt this is a safe area to go to.

heading to the castle. This created another problem, as along that main route I mentioned, the player is given two essential upgrades – getting Torrent the horse to speed up movement and have mounted combat, and access to the roundtable which acts as the hub complete with essential services.

In terms of progress, the game's difficulty felt a bit spikier compared to previous titles. As I said further up, the emphasis on the different ways of playing also factored into the boss fights. The final battle with the Elden Beast was notoriously difficult for people who only invested in melee builds, similar to the boss fight with Maliketh, The Black Blade.

For designers reading this, it's important at the start of an open-ended game to provide the player with the information they need to begin and provide a suitable point when you tell them, "Now you're on your own." I would have made the "essential path" shorter – stopping right after acquiring your horse. Instead of locking the roundtable to the bonfire right outside of Stormveil and the first official boss, make it unlock after the player visits any other new bonfire outside of the second one.

With that said, people still stuck with the game, I personally think due to the prestige factor of playing the new From Software game. One element that did work exclusively for *Elden Ring* was the freedom of exploration. Many AAA games tend to hold the player's hands to the point that it can feel like the game is not letting the player learn things on their own. *Elden Ring* exuded a confidence in its design that very few games had – with possibly *The Legend of Zelda Breath of the Wild* and *Tears of the Kingdom* (released in 2017 and 2023 by Nintendo) being similar. Once the player finished with the tutorial, that was it: they were set loose to explore the world. Where other AAA games overloaded the GUI with quest markets and other elements, the game went for a minimalistic design. For many people who didn't grow up playing **CRPGs**, this would be their first experience playing a game where they could look over the horizon, see something interesting or strange, and then head out there for an adventure. Many fans and critics equated playing *Elden Ring* to something of their childhood – a massive game where you could spend weeks or even months trying to find everything.

In one fell swoop, From Software managed to outdo not only every other soulslike on the market but the entire open-world genre at the same time. The last sales report at the time of writing this book by Bandai Namco in early 2023, put the game at over 20 million copies sold worldwide[1] and making it the most successful game From Software has put out to date.

It's a bit tricky to figure out what lessons we can take away from the success of *Elden Ring*. For designers reading this, I cannot stress enough the difference between a game and studio having clout vs. ones that don't. Even though *Elden Ring* was a great game, it did have issues with it, and those issues would have led to games with less notoriety behind them not doing anywhere near as good or people going into them in the first place.

One takeaway that is worth mentioning is the appeal of a game that gets out of its own way for the player to start getting into it. While the onboarding wasn't the best, *Elden Ring*, by AAA standards, had the shortest time from the title screen to letting the player get into it. Far too many AAA designers and games have approached the genre as a quasi-amusement park, where everything is just a heavily curated experience. The player is not allowed to explore off the beaten path for a long time, and when they are finally able to, there often isn't much in the way of interesting things to find. Proper onboarding and tutorial design is about giving the players what they need to know as quickly as possible so that they can start enjoying the game.

The world design as I mentioned draws similarities to the best CRPG and open-world games by presenting the player with 360° of freedom to explore, and usually having something in any direction. Many players would head east at the start of the game, as the roads naturally went that way, but instead of finding the next area to go to, they find one of the hardest sections in the form of Caelid. Caelid is a great lesson in terms of using aesthetics to inform the player about a place. Upon arriving, the sky turns blood red, and all grass and trees are replaced with dirt, rot, and dead trees (Figure 9.4). The common enemies in the area are of a higher tier compared to those in the previous area. The area itself is optional if someone just wants to do the main path and beat the game, but there are multiple side areas, gear and lore, and a major boss fight that can be found.

Elden Ring, represents an important aspect of being a game developer and a studio that goes to the heart of From Software as a company. There is a confidence in *Elden Ring*, much like all their previous soulslikes, that is hard to put

Figure 9.4

Caelid is one of the most interesting areas in all the soulslikes released. Everything about the area stands out from the rest of the game. Upon arriving, the player becomes uneasy at this strange land in front of them. It is also possible to trigger a trap in one of the earlier caves that will send the player's character to prison right in the middle of Caelid, which would be one of the biggest shocks in the game for new players.

into words. As I've talked about throughout this book, From Software as a studio has not really changed its long-form approach to game development. While things have improved from a UI/UX standpoint, the gameplay loops, systems, mechanics, and the aesthetics they are trying to evoke have remained consistent. Returning to *Demon's Souls*, it came out at a time when publishers and developers were thinking that people wanted easier games or games that weren't meant to be challenging, but *Demon's Souls* for the time, was the best representation of creating a challenging, but fair game. Today, that crown goes to *Elden Ring*, and could quite possibly represent the very heights of soulslike design for the remainder of the 2020s.

This is by no means telling you that just having confidence in your game is the magic secret to being a successful game designer. What you do need is to approach your games both with the passion to create them, and the goal of putting out the very best product that you can. When we look at the successes of niche designs, it does not happen overnight. Often, it takes word of mouth, a lot of **PR** work, and having something special for people to gravitate toward. And even then, that game can still fail in the market and a lot must go right for a game to be successful. Just looking at *Elden Ring* and thinking that if you copy the design, you will automatically succeed is the wrong lesson, and developers have tried this with every major design trend in the past 40 years.

Figure 9.5

Like From Software, it's easy to look at all of Nintendo's *Mario* games over the decade as just the same game, but each one provides something new and iterative on the formula. This is just a small snapshot of games, but Nintendo has gone back and forth over the years with new iterations being in 2D or 3D, Such as *Super Mario Bros. Wonder* which was released in 2023.

And if you think that you can go from having no gamedev background to creating an *Elden Ring*-sized experience as your first project, that's not going to happen either. Part of the growth that studios and developers have is being able to not only improve their processes but also refine their gameplay and design over years and on additional projects. Many new developers try to rush their "dream project," but it takes understanding what you and your studio can do and learning the tools that you have access to make something worthwhile, and no amount of studying or watching videos will help here – it only comes from experience. From Software could not go from *Demon's Souls* to *Elden Ring*, it took the entirety of the 2010s and improving and iterating on their design to get there; the same thing could be said of Nintendo and the evolution of the *Mario* franchise (Figure 9.5). And "iteration" is key here, another trap designers fall into is making the same game; maybe there's better art or more content, but it's the same game with the same mistakes time-after-time. Being able to learn and grow as a developer and as a studio is vital.

Elden Ring represents the culmination of From Software's soulslike design built over a decade, and how consumers are still looking for experiences to get lost in; without the designer constantly standing in the way of that. It is a game that is uniquely theirs, and why no other studio could have made a game like that today. It is a specialized game, from a specialized studio that wanted to make that specific design. In 2023, *Baldur's Gate 3* by Larian Studios became the year's biggest success, and again, is the culmination of a studio's philosophy and growth. This is not something that someone can just throw money at or get an education to create – it takes a lot of work.

9.2 Where Can Things Go from Here?

There are currently no plans as I'm writing this by From Software to work on a new soulslike or sequel to *Elden Ring*, and while that does leave the market open to other designers, it does make it difficult to talk about the future of this subgenre. The only other soulslike design to come in second as I talked about earlier is the greater focus on combat that the *Nioh* series has done. There are other games from smaller developers being released in 2023, but they are still in the older style, and not one currently is aiming to be open-world like *Elden Ring*.

Some games have experimented with making the combat more technical and complicated with combo moves and different rules for the weapons. It's an interesting strategy, as the original UI for *Demon's Souls* was put in to explicitly move away from the combat focus and button-intensive design of action games in the 2000s. And that is certainly one potential track, but it does present the possible issue of raising the skill curve even higher than before.

The idea of making more "casual soulslikes" is again where the game *Ashen* tried to go, but there is something intrinsic to soulslike design that separates it from a traditional action-based design. It's not about punishing the player or being outright difficult but rewarding the player's willingness to master the game. You can have a game that is easier to learn, but there still needs to be something "more" about the design that's worth pursuing (Figure 9.6). That some new area or new enemy waiting around the corner to test the player. If you can effectively master the game within a few minutes and there's nothing more to the gameplay loop, then that would be a game that fails as a soulslike. While it wasn't a soulslike by design, *Sekiro* did embody that philosophy – it is a game where the player must meet the design all the way. If the player failed to learn what the game expected out of them, there were no shortcuts or ways to circumvent it.

To wit, while it was originally viewed as a joke and marketing tactic by developers, creating the "*Dark Souls* of X" could theoretically work if handled properly. If a developer focuses too much on the lesson that a soulslike is meant to be overly difficult, then we end up with the slew of "rage games" I mentioned earlier. What I want to see is someone take the pacing and rewarding nature of a soulslike and translate that into another game genre. The reason why the *Remnant* series appealed to me is that it was the first time someone attempted to do this kind of design but in a third-person shooter format. One of my personal dream ideas is to create something with the push-forward design of *Doom Eternal* but having the pacing of a soulslike.

Regarding open-world design, the standard that *Elden Ring* set I feel is going to be it for some time, possibly for most of the 2020s, or at least until From Software decides to revisit the design (Figure 9.7). At the time of writing this, there is a planned DLC for the game that will expand things further.

Figure 9.6

Mystery and challenge go together with the best soulslike, the player should always be thinking about what the next threat is that's coming their way, and how they are going to respond to it. What *Elden Ring* did masterfully was take that question and give the player the freedom to decide what interesting thing on the horizon they're going to explore next.

Figure 9.7

Lies of P came out just as I was finishing the initial draft for the book and quickly succeeded thanks to its quality, story, aesthetics, and being one of the only major traditional soulslike released during the year. I personally doubt we will see a game comparative to *Elden Ring* by another studio in the next four years.

With that said, there is one area where From Software did not go with their games that can be capitalized on by other designers – improving the approachability and UI/UX. While there are lots of resources and examples of soulslikes that are aimed at a challenging experience, making one that provides affordances and quality of life features for more people is still not really seen. As of the end of 2023 and into 2024, people are looking for a new soulslike to jump into and *Lies of P* by NEOWIZ became successful as one of the only soulslikes to be released in 2023 along with *Remnant 2*.

Note

[1] https://www.forbes.com/sites/paultassi/2023/02/22/one-year-later-elden-ring-announces-20-million-copies-sold/?sh=47cd716e75d8

10

Conclusion

10.1 Why It's Harder Than It Looks to Make a Soulslike

This has been an interesting book to write and one of the surprisingly harder ones I've written. While the RPG book was much longer, this one felt the hardest to explain. Soulslikes may be the youngest genre I've covered, but it's very dense and specific in terms of its design. It is also the only genre to date where the defacto best games have all been from one developer, and even after a decade, no one has managed to beat From Software at their own game.

This is where the hurdle of designing a game in this genre comes from – as you are going to be competing with the studio and the games that have defined this design. However, I want you to understand that doesn't mean you are doomed right out of the gates.

During the 90s, the metroidvania subgenre was dominated by the *Castlevania* games developed by Konami, and no other major studio was even thinking of putting one out in fear of competing with and being compared to those games. Two things happened that would shift this market away from Konami – The studio stopped releasing metroidvania games, and indie developers would take the genre in new directions (Figure 10.1). It was no longer about trying to make a

DOI: 10.1201/9781003450078-10

Figure 10.1

Just trying to copy the biggest competitor in terms of design is not how you will succeed in any genre. Both *Nioh 2* and *Remnant 2* succeeded as sequels that stood separate from the From Software games. On the right, *Ori and the Will of the Wisps* and *Hollow Knight* (released in 2020 by Moon Studios GmbH and 2017 by Team Cherry respectively) were some of the bestselling metroidvanias by not trying to copy the ones that came before them.

game just like Konami but using that design as the template to try something new.

From Software did not invent action-RPG design, and as I talked about over the historical chapters, this design evolved as the industry did. Look at ways of taking the philosophy of soulslikes and putting that into a new design – imagine what a soulslike would look like with spaceships, giant robots, or anything else you can come up with. Just trying to create another *Dark Souls* or another *Elden Ring* is not going to change the genre or provide you with the same level of fame and notoriety.

I also want to make sure that you understand the differences between difficulty and challenge, as this is, no pun intended, a very hard concept to grasp by people. Being able to comprehend what aspects of something are challenging will help you when you are trying to balance your game and create something that is meant to push the player. It is not about just raising the difficulty of a game to extreme levels, nor can you achieve this by making everything easy. Good game designers explore their designs to create interesting challenges, not just those that are overly difficult. Making a soulslike is already going to present a challenging design and you cannot get away with the same difficulty spikes and pain points that are in From Software's titles. The finer points about developing and balancing the combat system can only come with experience and understanding. Much

Figure 10.2

You've made it to the very end of this book, and while I don't have access to the same font From Software uses, you at least deserve a bit of celebration for finishing a challenge.

like when I wrote about platforming and jumping, it's easy to assume because you've played lots of action games that you know what good combat is, but the feel is what separates the lesser soulslikes from the greats.

I would suggest for everyone reading this, if you are new to the industry or trying to pick a first game to make, I would not recommend making it a soulslike. This is one of the more advanced genres to build a game from and requires you to have a good understanding of both action and RPG design, and it's rare to find people who are good at both right from the start. In my RPG book, I specifically talked about how many designers have gone after the white whale of combining abstracted design with reflex-driven, and the hurdles that come with it. Making a good soulslike is not about designing a great RPG with poor combat or vice-versa but making both designs work in harmony together.

There are some advantages to making one that if you understand it right can help your game dev career. Due to the complexities of this design, making a good one will test your skills across multiple genres and gameplay loops. If you can create a soulslike that either stands next to, or in a way is better than, From Software's titles, that can be a major accolade for your studio and why many developers have made these games over the 2010s. The success of *Lies of P* has become a huge boost for NEOWIZ and one that they will be celebrating for some time. It also proves that there are still avenues for soulslike design – traditional or non, that you can explore with your game. And maybe one of you reading this could create the next *"Dark Souls of X"* that everyone can't stop talking about (Figure 10.2).

10. Conclusion

Glossary

AAA Used to describe major studios in the game industry such as Nintendo and Activision.

Aesthetics The emotion or mood a game is trying to convey using its art style, sound, and design.

Avatar Used to describe the player-created character that they control in a game.

CRPG Stands for "computer role playing game" and is a style of RPG that focuses on creating a customized character or characters and exploring the land.

DLC Stands for "downloadable content" and is any additional content developed and released for the game as a separate purchase and installation after the game's launch.

GUI Short for "graphical user interface" and is a catchall term for all on-screen elements and menus that someone will be looking at to understand what is going on in a video game.

Hitbox An invisible box that surrounds character models and physical projectiles. If an attack hitbox connects with the player character's hitbox, then the game will consider that a hit.

I-Frame Short for "invincibility frames" and represents frames of animation that a character is immune to all incoming damage.

IP Short for "intellectual property" and for video games represents branding – either the studio's brand or working with someone else's property to make a game licensed off of it.

Metroidvania A type of game that focuses on the player unlocking new abilities that change how they move through the world and progress. Typically, it is 2D, but there are exceptions.

MMOG	Stands for "massively multiplayer online game" and is a genre built around players exploring and interacting in a virtual world alongside everyone else.
NPC	Short for "nonplayable character" and refers to characters that exist in a game that aren't controlled by any player.
PR	Short for "public relations" and for videogames represents the marketing, networking, and getting word out about a game's release.
Respec	The option in a game to completely reset a player's character and let them rebuild them in a different way.
RPG	Short for "role playing game," a kind of game that focuses on abstracted elements and attributes as opposed to reflex-based design.
Skill floor	The skill level required by the player of a game to be able to start playing it.
Soulslike	A popular game genre built on challenging gameplay that mixes action and RPG design.
Systems	A collection of game mechanics that all are part of the same gameplay loop.
UI	Short for "user interface" and is a catchall term to describe how someone interacts with a video game. Often paired with the graphical user interface or "GUI" to describe the on-screen elements that someone will be looking at.
UX	Short for "user experience" and is a catchall term to describe what it feels like to play a video game. Goes hand-in-hand with UI and the two affect the playability and approachability of a video game.

Index

Note: *Italic* page numbers refer to figures.

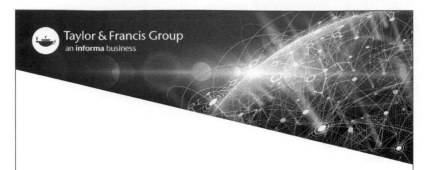